Disclaimer

Although every effort has been made to provide complete and accurate information, there are no warranties, expressed or implied, or representations as to the accuracy of content in this book. No liability or responsibility for any error or omissions in the information contained in this book is assumed.

Contents

Hello folks and welcome to British Top 20 Hits of the 1950's.

I'm a music collector and I've collected many of the publications that have been generated on the subject. What I found however, was a lack of easy to read information on the subject of just top 20 chart hits. With this in mind I set about producing just that - an easy to read, practical listing of every British top 20 single from 1952, when it all began, to 1959.

There are many excellent publications that can provide you with all kinds of details concerning the date that a particular single first entered the UK chart, the label it was released on, the catalogue number etc., and I don't believe that I would have added any value to you by repeating that information here. On the contrary, rather than repeat what is already available I've tried to provide something which is not, and that is a clear listing of every single artist and title that occupied a top 20 position in the British chart in a particular year, the highest position that the single reached in that year, and the week ending (W/E) date of the chart in which that position was reached. As you read through the charts you'll see that the information has been laid out in chronological chart-date order, starting with January and moving on through to December. You should note that there are a small number of occasions when you will not find any chart movements listed for the last week of the year. **This is not an error** - the reason is simply because there were no chart movements listed in the last chart of the year and therefore all entries remained in their previous positions as shown in the chart of the previous week.

In addition to the chart information that has been compiled by year, and to make life easier for you, I've added an **alphabetical list by artist** of every top 20 hit for the decade, and an **alphabetical list by title** of every top 20 hit for the decade. Finally, I've tried to provide you with a flavour of each of the years by including a little light-hearted trivia on some of the events of the day.

I do hope that you derive as much knowledge and entertainment from the finished article as I did putting it all together!

For details of other books available in this series please visit
www.BritishTop20Hits.com

Enjoy...........

Nick

Thanks & acknowledgements

With sincere thanks to Natalia, Gregory and Andrew for your patience and understanding.

Who knows, you guys might even find this useful one day! ☺

My love to you all

1950 & 1951

Welcome to the lighter side of life in Britain in the early 1950's

The Early 1950"s

By the time we reached the end of 1952 and the advent of the very first British Singles Chart there had already been a number of key events that had gripped the nation!

The events...........

- The Princess Elizabeth had given birth to Princess Anne Elizabeth Alice Louise[1]
- Full-time military service by conscripted National Servicemen had been extended to two years[7]
- The rebuilt House of Commons, following its destruction by bombing in World War II, had been used for the first time[15]
- The Stone of Scone, the traditional coronation stone of Scottish monarchs, English monarchs and more recently British monarchs, had been stolen from London's Westminster Abbey by a group of four Scottish students, and found later in Forfar, Scotland[15]

Stone of Scone Replica
© BUBOBUBO2 (2009) / Wikimedia
Commons / CC BY-SA 3.0

- The Peak District had been established as the first of the national parks of England and Wales, followed by the Lake District, Snowdonia and Dartmoor shortly afterwards[7]
- George VI had opened the Festival of Britain in London, including the Royal Festival Hall, Dome of Discovery, and Skylon[2]
- The Conservative Party under Winston Churchill had won the 1951 general election[3]
- At 10-storey high, The Lawn, in Harlow New Town had become the first residential tower block construction in Britain[4,5,6]

In the world of sport......

- The World Figure Skating Championships had been held in London[7]
- The first Grand Prix had been held at Silverstone[8]

- The football World Cup had opened in Brazil with the England national team competing for the first time[13]
- Boxer Randy Turpin had beaten Sugar Ray Robinson in London to become the World Middleweight Champion[7]
- The England cricket team had lost the Test Match with the West Indies by 326 runs[13]
- Warwickshire's Eric Hollies had beaten Nobby Clark's record of 65 innings without reaching double figures when dismissed for 7 against Worcestershire. Hollies would eventually make it 71 innings before scoring 14 against Nottinghamshire in August of 1950[7]
- The Football League had increased its membership from 88 to 92 clubs across the four divisions[9]
- Vale Park football stadium had opened in Stoke-on-Trent to serve Port Vale F.C. with an initial capacity of more than 30,000[10]

Statue of Randolph Turpin
© Ethendra (2006) / Wikimedia Commons /
CC BY-SA 3.0

- Arsenal had won the 1950 FA Cup with a 2-0 win over Liverpool at Wembley Stadium[7]
- Newcastle United had won the 1951 FA Cup for the fourth time with a 2-0 win over Blackpool at Wembley Stadium[11]
- Workington F.C. had been elected to the Football League in place of A.F.C. Brighton[12]

In the world of entertainment…….

- The daily children's radio feature *"Listen With Mother"* had been introduced by the BBC[13]
- The *"Eagle"* comic had first appeared featuring *Dan Dare & Captain Pugwash*[13]
- *"Andy Pandy"* had first appeared on our TV screens[15]
- The first Miss World beauty pageant had been held in London[14]
- The pilot episode of *"The Archers"* had been first broadcast on BBC Radio – who would have guessed that it would still be running more than 60 years later![15]
- The "X" rating for films had been first introduced by the British Board of Film Censors[7]
- *"The Gambols"* comic strip had first appeared in the *Daily Express*[13]
- The popular radio comedy feature *Educating Archie,* with Max Bygraves had been first brought to the air by the BBC[13]
- The BBC had made its first television broadcast from the European continent[15]

- The Festival Ballet, later to become the English National Ballet had made its debut performance[16],[17]
- "Dennis the Menace" had first appeared in the *Beano* comic[13]
- The C.S. Lewis novel *The Lion, the Witch and the Wardrobe*, first of *The Chronicles of Narnia* series had been published[18]
- John Wyndham's novel *The Day of the Triffids* had been published[7]
- The first broadcast of *The Goon Show* radio series had taken place[15]
- Walt Disney's 13th animated film, *Alice in Wonderland*, had premiered in London[19]

In the world of business.....

- Sainsbury's had opened its first supermarket in Croydon, Surrey[20]
- Post-war soap rationing had come to an end[20]
- Ferranti had delivered the first commercially available general purpose computer to the University of Manchester[21]
- The Kenwood Chef food mixer had been introduced[7]
- Express Dairies, owned by 28-year-old Paul Galvani, had opened Britain's first full-size supermarket in Streatham Hill, London[22]
- LEO had become the world's first computer to run a full commercial business application, for the baker J. Lyons and Co.[23]
- Trade union membership had reached an all-time peak, with 9.3 million members[13]

Ford Consul MkII (204E)
© Simon GP Geohagen (2007) / Wikimedia Commons CC BY 3.0

In the world of education............

- GCE O & A levels had been introduced[7]

In the world of transport ....

- Motor fuel rationing had come to an end after 11 years[24]
- The Ford Consul motor car had been introduced[7]
- Zebra crossings had been introduced[15]
- The Austin A30 motor car had been introduced[7]

Picture of Abbey Road Zebra Crossing in London
© WillMcC (2006) / Wikimedia Commons CC BY-SA 3.0

1954 Austin A30
Credit: Adrian Pingstone (2004) / Wikimedia Commons / Public Domain

7

1952

Wow - what a start to a new decade that was about to get even better with the establishment of the very first British Singles Chart ever!

The music…..

Artist	Title	Highest position this year	W/E date
Al Martino	Here in my heart	1	20-Nov
Doris Day & Frankie Laine	Sugarbush	8	20-Nov
Frankie Laine	High noon (do not forsake me)	7	20-Nov
Jo Stafford	You belong to me	2	20-Nov
Johnny Ray	Walkin' my baby back home	12	20-Nov
Max Bygraves	Cowpuncher's cantata	11	20-Nov
Nat 'King' Cole	Somewhere along the way	3	20-Nov
Ray Martin	Blue Tango	8	20-Nov
Vera Lynn	The homing waltz	9	20-Nov
Vera Lynn	Auf wiederseh'n sweetheart	10	20-Nov
Al Martino	Take my heart	9	27-Nov
Doris Day	My love and devotion	10	27-Nov
Guy Mitchell	Feet up (pat him on the po-po)	2	27-Nov
Rosemary Clooney	Half as much	3	27-Nov
Bing Crosby & Jane Wyman	Zing a little zing	10	11-Dec
Mario Lanza	Because you're mine	3	11-Dec
Bing Crosby	The Isle of Innisfree	3	18-Dec
Vera Lynn	Forget me not	5	18-Dec
Winifred Atwell	Britannia rag	11	18-Dec
Bing Crosby	Silent night	8	25-Dec
Jo Stafford	Jambalaya	11	25-Dec

Johnnie Ray & The Four Lads	Faith can move mountains	7	25-Dec
Kay Starr	Comes-a-long-a-love	3	25-Dec
Louis Armsrong	Takes two to tango	8	25-Dec
Mantovani	White Christmas	6	25-Dec
Nat 'King' Cole	Because you're mine	6	25-Dec
Tony Brent	Walkin' to Missouri	9	25-Dec

So whilst these tracks were filling the airwaves of the day, here is a list of some of the events that would have been filling the newspapers of the day:

The events............

- 25 year old Elizabeth was proclaimed as Queen Elizabeth II[25]
- The Great Smog blanketed London[26]
- Compulsory identity cards, issued during World War II, were abandoned[25]
- Churchill announced that the United Kingdom had an atomic bomb[27]
- Reindeer were re-introduced to the Cairngorms of Scotland[28]
  A one shilling charge was introduced for prescription drugs dispensed under the National Health Service[29]

In the world of sport ......

- Great Britain and Northern Ireland competed at the Winter Olympics in Oslo and won one gold, 2 silver and 8 bronze medals[27]
- Len Hutton was appointed as the England cricket team's first professional captain for 65 years[30]
- Newcastle United won the FA Cup with a 1-0 win over Arsenal at Wembley Stadium[31]

Queen Elizabeth II and Prince Philip, Duke of Edinburgh. Coronation portrait June 1953
Credit: Cecil Beaton / Wikimedia Commons / Public Domain

In the world of entertainment.......

- NME Magazine published the first UK Singles Chart[25]
- The first appearance of Sooty took place on BBC Television[30]
- The first broadcast of The Flower Pot Men took place[27]
- Agatha Christie's play, The Mousetrap, opened in London[32]

- The first TV detector van was commissioned in a bid to clamp down on an estimated 150,000 unlicensed TV sets[33]

In the world of business.....

- Tea rationing ended after 13 years[34],[35]
- Geoffrey Dummer proposed the Integrated Circuit[36]
- The *Manchester Guardian* printed news, rather than advertisements, on its front page for the first time[27]

In the world of transport.....

- The De Havilland Comet became the world's first jet airliner with a maiden flight from London to Johannesburg[27]
- The last of the original trams ran in London[37]

London United Tramways double deck tram in 1910
Wikimedia Commons / Public Domain

1953

Welcome to the lighter side of life in Britain in 1953

The music........

Artist	Title	Highest position this year	W/E date
Al Martino	Here in my heart	1	01-Jan
Bing Crosby	The Isle of Innisfree	3	01-Jan
Guy Mitchell	Feet up	4	01-Jan
Rosemary Clooney	Half as much	5	01-Jan
Nat 'King' Cole	Somewhere along the way	6	01-Jan
Mantovani Orchestra	White Christmas	6	01-Jan
Nat 'King' Cole	Because you're mine	6	01-Jan
Johnnie Ray & The Four Lads	Faith can move mountains	7	01-Jan
Bing Crosby	Silent night	8	01-Jan
Vera Lynn	Forget me not	10	01-Jan
Doris Day & Frankie Laine	Sugarbush	10	01-Jan
Jo Stafford	Jambalaya	11	01-Jan
Frankie Laine	High noon (do not forsake me)	12	01-Jan
Tony Brent	Walkin' to Missouri	7	15-Jan
Mills Brothers	Glow worm	10	15-Jan
Jimmy Young	Faith can move mountains	11	15-Jan
Jo Stafford	You belong to me	1	22-Jan
Mario Lanza	Because you're mine	3	22-Jan
Tony Brent	Make it soon	9	22-Jan
Ted Heath & His Music	Vanessa	11	22-Jan
Winifred Atwell	Britannia rag	5	29-Jan
Kay Starr	Comes a-long-a-love	1	29-Jan
Louis Armstrong	It takes two to tango	6	29-Jan
Max Bygraves	Cowpuncher's cantata	6	29-Jan

11

Tony Brent	Got you on my mind	12	29-Jan
Eddie Fisher	Outside of Heaven	1	05-Feb
Nat 'King' Cole	Faith can move mountains	10	12-Feb
Perry Como	Don't let the stars get in your eyes	1	12-Feb
Eddie Fisher	Everything I have is yours	8	12-Feb
Dickie Valentine	Broken wings	12	26-Feb
Art & Dotty Todd	Broken wings	6	05-Mar
Joni James	Why don't you believe me?	11	12-Mar
Guy Mitchell	She wears red feathers	1	19-Mar
Al Martino	Now	3	26-Mar
Dickie Valentine	All the time and everywhere	9	26-Mar
Frankie Laine	The girl in the wood	11	26-Mar
Buddy Morrow	Night train	12	26-Mar
Patti Page	How much is that doggie in the window?	9	02-Apr
Frank Chacksfield's Tunesmiths	Little red monkey	10	09-Apr
Doris Day & Johnnie Ray	Ma says, Pa says	12	09-Apr
Stargazers	Broken wings	1	16-Apr
Danny Kaye	Wonderful Copenhagen	5	16-Apr
Johnnie Ray	Somebody stole my gal	6	16-Apr
Lita Roza	How much is that doggie in the window?	1	23-Apr
Doris Day & Johnnie Ray	Full time job	11	23-Apr
Frankie Laine	I believe	1	30-Apr
Johnston Brothers	Oh happy day	4	07-May
Guy Mitchell	Pretty little black eyed Susie	2	07-May
Kay Starr	Side by side	7	07-May
Nat 'King' Cole	Pretend	2	14-May
Frankie Laine & Jimmy Boyd	Tell me a story	5	21-May
Eddie Fisher	Downhearted	3	28-May

Billy Cotton & His Band	In a golden coach	3	11-Jun
Winifred Atwell	Coronation rag	5	11-Jun
Frank Chacksfield	Terry's theme from 'Limelight'	2	11-Jun
Dickie Valentine	In a golden coach	7	11-Jun
Vera Lynn	The Windsor waltz	11	11-Jun
Dorothy Squires	I'm walking behind you	12	11-Jun
Muriel Smith	Hold me, thrill me, kiss me	3	25-Jun
Eddie Fisher & Sally Sweetland	I'm walking behind you	1	02-Jul
Al Martino	Rachel	10	16-Jul
Vivian Blaine	A bushel and a peck	12	16-Jul
Ron Goodwin	Terry's theme from 'Limelight'	3	13-Aug
Mantovani Orchestra	Theme from 'Moulin Rouge'	1	20-Aug
Ted Heath & His Music	Hot toddy	6	20-Aug
Gisele McKenzie	Seven lonely days	6	03-Sep
Doris Day & Johnnie Ray	Let's walk that-a-way	4	03-Sep
Jimmy Young	Eternally	8	10-Sep
Guy Mitchell	Look at that girl	1	17-Sep
Jane Hutton & Axel Stordahl	Say you're mine again	6	24-Sep
Nat 'King' Cole	Can't I?	6	01-Oct
David Whitfield	Bridge of sighs	9	08-Oct
Frankie Laine	Where the winds blow	2	08-Oct
Winifred Atwell	Flirtation waltz	10	15-Oct
Nat 'King' Cole	Mother Nature and Father Time	7	22-Oct
Dean Martin	Kiss	5	29-Oct
Frankie Laine	Hey Joe	1	29-Oct
David Whitfield	Answer me	1	12-Nov
Frankie Laine	Answer me	1	19-Nov
Eddie Fisher	Wish you were here	8	26-Nov
Les Paul & Mary Ford	Vaya con dios	7	26-Nov

Ted Heath & His Music	Dragnet	9	03-Dec
Mantovani Orchestra	Swedish Rhapsody	2	10-Dec
Jimmy Boyd	I saw Mommy kissing Santa Claus	3	10-Dec
Ray Anthony & His Orchestra	Dragnet	7	10-Dec
Diana Decker	Poppa Piccolino	2	17-Dec
Guy Mitchell	Chick-a-boom	5	17-Dec
Lee Lawrence	Crying in the chapel	7	17-Dec
Beverley Sisters	I saw Mommy kissing Santa Claus	6	17-Dec
Winifred Atwell	Let's have a party	3	17-Dec
Joan Regan	Ricochet	8	17-Dec
David Whitfield	Rags to riches	12	17-Dec
Ray Martin Concert Orchestra	Swedish Rhapsody	4	24-Dec
Eddie Calvert	Oh mein Papa	6	24-Dec
Billy Cotton & His Band	I saw Mommy kissing Santa Claus	11	24-Dec
Guy Mitchell	Cloud lucky seven	12	24-Dec

The events........

- The Samaritans telephone counselling service was started by Rev. Chad Varah in London[49]
- Sugar rationing ended[38]
- Winston Churchill received a knighthood from the Queen[39]
- Eskdalemuir entered the UK Weather Records for the highest rainfall in a 30-minute period with 80mm[49]
- The Piltdown Man, which was discovered in 1912 and thought to be the fossilised remains of a hitherto unknown form of early human, was exposed as a hoax[39]
- Sweet rationing ended[40]

In the world of sport ......

- 21 year old centre forward Tommy Taylor became Britain's most expensive footballer in a £29,999 transfer from Barnsley United[41],[42]
- Blackpool won the first ever televised FA Cup final with a 4-3 victory over Bolton Wanderers[43],[44]

Sir Winston Churchill
Credit: UN Information Office, New York (1942) / Wikimedia Commons / Public Domain

14

- Gordon Richards became the only jockey to be made a knight[45]
- The England cricket team under Len Hutton defeated Australia to win The Ashes for the first time in 19 years[39]
- The England football team was defeated by Hungary 6-3 at Wembley Stadium, ending a 90-year unbeaten home run against sides from outside the British Isles[49]

In the world of entertainment.......

- Ian Fleming published the first James Bond novel, *"Casino Royale"*[46]
- *The Quatermass Experiment,* first of the *Quatermass* science-fiction serials by Nigel Kneale, began its run on BBC Television[49]
- *The Good Old Days* began its 30-year run on BBC Television[49]
- The current affairs series *Panorama* was first aired on BBC Television[39]
- The House of Lords voted in favour of the government's proposals for commercial television[47]

The first mass produced TV set, sold 1946-47
© Matthew Hill (2012)
Wikimedia Commons / CC BY-SA 3.0 Unported

- Some 25% of British households were now reported to own a television set, 17 years after the first sets became available[48]
- John Wyndham's novel *The Kraken Wakes* was published[49]

In the world of business.....

- James D. Watson and Francis Crick announced that they had discovered the structure of the DNA molecule[49]
- The first Italian espresso bar, The Moka, opened in Frith Street, Soho, London[50]
- Matchbox toy vehicles were introduced by Lesney Products of London[49]

In the world of transport.....

- The Queen launched the Royal Yacht *Britannia* at John Brown & Company shipbuilders on the Clyde[51]
- The first roll-on/roll-off ferry crossing of the English Channel took place, between Dover and Boulogne[52]

1954

Welcome to the lighter side of life in Britain in 1954

The music.......

Artist	Title	Highest position this year	W/E date
Frankie Laine	Answer me	1	07-Jan
David Whitfield	Answer me	2	07-Jan
Ray Martin	Swedish Rhapsody	4	07-Jan
Beverley Sisters	I saw Mommy kissing Santa Claus	7	07-Jan
Jimmy Boyd	I saw Mommy kissing Santa Claus	8	07-Jan
Lee Lawrence	Crying in the chapel	10	07-Jan
Billy Cotton Band	I saw Mommy kissing Santa Claus	11	07-Jan
Eddie Fisher	Wish you were here	12	07-Jan
Mantovani Orchestra	Swedish Rhapsody	2	14-Jan
Eddie Calvert	Oh mein Papa	1	14-Jan
David Whitfield	Rags to riches	3	14-Jan
Diana Decker	Poppa Piccolino	5	14-Jan
Ray Anthony	Dragnet	11	14-Jan
Winifred Atwell	Let's have a party	2	21-Jan
Frankie Laine	Blowing wild	2	21-Jan
Ted Heath & His Music	Dragnet	11	21-Jan
Eddie Fisher	Oh my papa	9	28-Jan
Guy Mitchell	Chick-a-boom	4	04-Feb
Joan Regan	Ricochet	9	04-Feb
Ken Mackintosh	The creep	10	04-Feb
Frankie Vaughan	Istanbul (not Constantinople)	11	04-Feb
Guy Mitchell	Cloud lucky seven	2	18-Feb
Bonnie Lou	Tennessee wig walk	4	18-Feb
Frank Chacksfield	Ebb tide	9	18-Feb
Dean Martin	That's amore	2	25-Feb

Rosemary Clooney & Jose Ferrer	Man / Woman	7	25-Feb
Ted Heath & His Music	Skin deep	9	25-Feb
Guy Mitchell	The cuff of my shirt	9	25-Feb
Guy Mitchell	Sippin' soda	11	04-Mar
Stargazers	I see the moon	1	18-Mar
Duke Ellington	Skin deep	7	18-Mar
Glenn Miller	Moonlight serenade	12	18-Mar
Obernkirchen Children's Choir	The happy wanderer	2	25-Mar
David Whitfield	The book	5	01-Apr
Bing Crosby	Changing partners	9	08-Apr
Alma Cogan	Bell bottom blues	4	08-Apr
Norman Wisdom	Don't laugh at me ('cause I'm a fool)	3	15-Apr
Kay Starr	Changing partners	4	15-Apr
Frankie Laine	Granada	9	15-Apr
Stargazers	The happy wanderer	12	15-Apr
Doris Day	Secret love	1	22-Apr
Nat 'King' Cole	Tenderly	10	22-Apr
Johnnie Ray	Such a night	1	06-May
Frankie Laine	The kid's last fight	3	06-May
Guy Mitchell	A dime and a dollar	8	06-May
Ruby Wright	Bimbo	7	13-May
Jo Stafford	Make love to me	8	13-May
Billy Cotton Band	Friends and neighbours	3	27-May
Max Bygraves	(The gang that sang) Heart of my heart	7	03-Jun
Joan Regan	Someone else's roses	5	10-Jun
Perry Como	Wanted	4	24-Jun
Four Knights	(Oh baby mine) I get so lonely	5	01-Jul
David Whitfield with Mantovani & His Orchestra	Cara Mia	1	08-Jul
Frank Sinatra	Young at heart	12	15-Jul
Al Martino	Wanted	4	29-Jul
Petula Clark	The little shoemaker	7	29-Jul
Four Aces	Three coins in the fountain	5	19-Aug

Perry Como	Idle gossip	3	26-Aug
Winifred Atwell	The story of three loves (Rachmaninoff's 18th variation on a theme by Paganini)	9	02-Sep
Doris Day	The black hills of Dakota	7	02-Sep
Alma Cogan	Little things mean a lot	11	02-Sep
Kitty Kallen	Little things mean a lot	1	16-Sep
Frank Sinatra	Three coins in the fountain	1	23-Sep
Frankie Laine	My friend	3	30-Sep
Max Bygraves	Gilly Gilly Ossenfeffer Katzenellen Bogen By The Sea	7	30-Sep
Anthony Steel & the Radio Revellers	West of Zanzibar	11	30-Sep
Ronnie Harris	The story of Tina	12	30-Sep
Nat 'King' Cole	Smile	2	07-Oct
Al Martino	The story of Tina	10	07-Oct
Don Cornell	Hold my hand	1	14-Oct
Crew Cuts	Sh-boom	12	14-Oct
Nat 'King' Cole	Make her mine	11	14-Oct
Dean Martin	Sway	6	21-Oct
Kay Starr	Am I a toy or a treasure?	17	21-Oct
Frankie Laine	There must be a reason	9	28-Oct
Dean Martin	How do you speak to an angel?	15	28-Oct
Billie Anthony	This ole house	4	04-Nov
Frankie Laine & The Four Lads	Rain, rain, rain	8	04-Nov
Vera Lynn	My son, my son	1	11-Nov
Dickie Valentine	Endless	19	11-Nov
Joan Regan & The Johnston Brothers	Wait for me darling	18	11-Nov
Doris Day & the Mellomen	If I give my heart to you	4	18-Nov
Norman Brooks	A sky blue shirt and a rainbow tie	17	18-Nov
Stan Freberg	Sh-boom	15	25-Nov
Rosemary Clooney	This ole house	1	02-Dec

18

Joan Regan	If I give my heart to you	3	02-Dec
Eddie Fisher	I need you now	13	09-Dec
David Whitfield	Santo Natale	2	09-Dec
Winifred Atwell	Let's have another party	1	09-Dec
Billy Eckstine	No-one but you	4	16-Dec
Perry Como	Papa loves mambo	16	16-Dec
Ronnie Hilton	I still believe	3	23-Dec
Ruby Murray	Heartbeat	10	23-Dec
Alma Cogan	I can't tell a waltz from a tango	14	23-Dec
Big Ben Banjo Band	Let's get together No.1	6	23-Dec
Ronnie Hilton	Veni vidi vici	16	23-Dec
Dickie Valentine	The finger of suspicion	7	23-Dec
Chordettes	Mr. Sandman	17	23-Dec
Bill Haley & His Comets	Shake, rattle and roll	13	23-Dec
Dickie Valentine	Mr. Sandman	19	23-Dec
Rosemary Clooney & The Mellomen	Mambo Italiano	20	23-Dec
Charlie Kunz	Piano medley No. 114	20	23-Dec

The events………..

- Britain witnessed its first eclipse since 1927 as the eclipse in America cast its shadow over Europe and Asia[53]
- Donald McGill, the artist of saucy seaside postcards, was found guilty of breaching the Obscene Publications Act 1857[54]
- Winston Churchill became the first British Prime Minister to reach his 80th birthday whilst still in office[59]

Total solar eclipse
© Luc Viatour (1999) /
www.Lucnix.be
Wikimedia Commons /
CC BY-SA 3.0 Unported

In the world of sport ……

- Roger Bannister became the first person to break the 4-minute mile at the Iffley Road Track at the University of Oxford[55]
- Oxford won the 100th Boat Race[56]
- Wolverhampton Wanderers won the Football League First Division title for the first time in their history[57]
- Chris Chataway broke the world record for the 5,000 metres by 5 seconds[58]

- West Bromwich Albion won the FA Cup for the fourth time in their history with a 3-2 win over Preston North End at Wembley Stadium[59]
- Diane Leather became the first woman to break the 5-minute mile, at the Alexander Sports Ground in Birmingham[60],[61]
- The Great Britain national rugby team beat France to win the first Rugby League World Cup at the Parc des Princes in Paris[59]

In the world of entertainment.......

- BBC Television broadcasted the opening episode of *The Grove Family*, the first British TV soap opera[62]
- The radio comedy series *Hancock's Half Hour* was first aired[68]
- Ian Fleming's James Bond novel *Live and Let Die* was published[59]
- William Golding's novel *Lord of the Flies* was published[59]
- The UK Singles Chart was expanded into a Top20[63]
- J.R.R. Tolkien's *The Fellowship of the Ring* and *The Two Towers*, the first two volumes of *The Lord of the Rings* were published[59]

In the world of business.....

- Fourteen years of rationing during and following World War II came to an end when meat officially came off ration[64]
- The first UK Wimpy bar was opened at the Lyons Corner House in Coventry Street, London[65]
- The United Kingdom Atomic Energy Authority was founded[66]

In the world of education.....

- Kidbrooke School in the London Borough of Greenwich opened as Britain's first purpose-built comprehensive school[67]

In the world of transport.....

- The maiden flight of the English Electric Lightning P-1 supersonic fighter plane took place[68]

English Electric Lightning P-1
Credit: AR Pingstone (1964)
Wikimedia Commons / Public
Domain

1955

Welcome to the lighter side of life in Britain in 1955

The music……..

Artist	Title	Highest position this year	W/E date
Winifred Atwell	Let's have another party	1	06-Jan
David Whitfield	Santo Natale	2	06-Jan
Ronnie Hilton	I still believe	3	06-Jan
Rosemary Clooney	This ole house	4	06-Jan
Big Ben Banjo Band	Let's get together No.1	6	06-Jan
Vera Lynn	My son, my son	8	06-Jan
Billie Anthony	This ole house	12	06-Jan
Joan Regan	If I give me heart to you	14	06-Jan
Eddie Fisher	I need you now	18	06-Jan
Winifred Atwell	Let's have a party	20	06-Jan
Dickie Valentine	The finger of suspicion	1	13-Jan
Don Cornell	Hold my hand	7	13-Jan
Chordettes	Mr.Sandman	11	13-Jan
Billy Eckstine	No one but you	3	20-Jan
Rosemary Clooney &The Mellomen	Mambo Italiano	1	20-Jan
Charlie Kunz	Piano medley No. 114	16	20-Jan
Four Aces	Mr.Sandman	9	20-Jan
Frankie Laine & The Four Lads	Rain, rain, rain	8	27-Jan
Bill Haley & His Comets	Shake, rattle and roll	4	27-Jan
Alma Cogan	I can't tell a waltz from a tango	6	27-Jan
Suzi Miller & The Johnston Brothers	Happy days and lonely nights	14	27-Jan
Max Bygraves	Mr.Sandman	16	27-Jan
Ruby Murray	Heartbeat	3	03-Feb

Ronnie Hilton	Veni, vidi, vici	12	03-Feb
Bing Crosby	Count your blessings instead of sheep	11	03-Feb
Dickie Valentine	Mr.Sandman	5	10-Feb
Frankie Vaughan	Happy days and lonely nights	12	10-Feb
Mario Lanza	The drinking song	13	10-Feb
Dean Martin	Mambo Italiano	14	10-Feb
Ames Brothers	The naughty lady of Shady Lane	6	17-Feb
Mantovani	Lonely ballerina	16	17-Feb
De Castro Sisters	Teach me tonight	20	17-Feb
Ruby Murray	Softly, softly	1	24-Feb
Teresa Brewer & The Lancers	Let me go lover	9	24-Feb
Joan Weber	Let me go lover	16	24-Feb
Mario Lanza	I'll walk with God	18	24-Feb
Ruby Murray	Happy days and lonely nights	6	03-Mar
Dean Martin	The naughty lady of Shady Lane	5	10-Mar
David Whitfield & Mantovani	Beyond the stars	8	10-Mar
Petula Clark	Majorca	12	10-Mar
Stargazers	Somebody	20	10-Mar
Tennessee Ernie Ford	Give me your word	1	17-Mar
Frankie Laine	In the beginning	20	17-Mar
Ray Burns	Mobile	4	24-Mar
Nat 'King' Cole	A blossom fell	3	24-Mar
Ruby Murray	Let me go lover	5	24-Mar
Dickie Valentine	A blossom fell	9	31-Mar
Dean Martin	Let me go lover	3	31-Mar
Johnny Brandon & The Phantoms	Tomorrow	8	31-Mar
Eddie Fisher	(I'm always hearing) Wedding bells	5	07-Apr
McGuire Sisters	No more	20	07-Apr
Ronnie Hilton	A blossom fell	10	14-Apr
Ruby Murray & Anne Warren	If anyone finds this, I love you	4	14-Apr
Joan Regan	Prize of gold	6	14-Apr

Dean Martin	Under the bridges of Paris	6	21-Apr
Doris Day	Ready, willing and able	7	21-Apr
Bill Haley & His Comets	Mambo rock	14	21-Apr
Eartha Kitt	Under the bridges of Paris	7	28-Apr
Frankie Vaughan	Tweedle dee	17	28-Apr
Georgia Gibbs	Tweedle dee	20	28-Apr
Perez Prado	Cherry pink and apple blossom white	1	05-May
Tony Martin	Stranger in Paradise	6	05-May
Don Cornell	Stranger in Paradise	19	05-May
Mario Lanza	Serenade	15	12-May
Ink Spots	Melody of love	10	12-May
Bing Crosby	Stranger in Paradise	17	12-May
Joan & Rusty Regan	Open up your heart	19	12-May
Tony Bennett	Stranger in Paradise	1	19-May
Crew Cuts	Earth angel	4	19-May
Johnnie Ray	If you believe	7	26-May
Johnnie Ray	Paths of Paradise	20	26-May
Eddie Calvert	Cherry pink and apple blossom white	1	02-Jun
Les Baxter & His Orchestra	Unchained melody	10	02-Jun
Eddie Calvert	Stranger in Paradise	14	02-Jun
Four Aces	Stranger in Paradise	6	09-Jun
Al Hibbler	Unchained melody	2	16-Jun
Joe 'Mr.Piano' Henderson	Sing it with Joe	14	16-Jun
Stargazers	The Crazy Otto rag	18	16-Jun
Frank Sinatra	You my love	13	16-Jun
Judy Garland	The man that got away	18	23-Jun
Liberace	Unchained melody	20	23-Jun
Jimmy Young	Unchained melody	1	30-Jun
Rosemary Clooney & The Mellomen	Where will the dimple be?	6	30-Jun
Jane Froman	I wonder	14	07-Jul
Alma Cogan	Dreamboat	1	21-Jul
Dickie Valentine	I wonder	4	21-Jul
McGuire Sisters	Sincerely	14	21-Jul

Cyril Stapleton	Elephant tango	19	28-Jul
Barbara Lyon	Stowaway	12	28-Jul
Ruby Murray	Evermore	3	28-Jul
Johnny Brandon	Don't worry	18	28-Jul
Five Smith Brothers	I'm in favour of friendship	20	28-Jul
Slim Whitman	Rose Marie	1	04-Aug
Frankie Laine & The Mellomen	Cool water	2	11-Aug
Frankie Laine	Strange lady in town	6	18-Aug
Ferko String Band	Alabama jubilee	20	18-Aug
David Whitfield	Mama	12	25-Aug
Slim Whitman	Indian love call	7	01-Sep
Frank Sinatra	Learnin' the blues	2	01-Sep
Malcolm Vaughan	Every day of my life	5	08-Sep
Eddie Calvert	John and Julie	6	08-Sep
Sammy Davis Jr.	Something's gotta give	11	08-Sep
Frank Sinatra	Not as a stranger	18	08-Sep
Ronnie Hilton	Stars shine in your eyes	13	15-Sep
Joe 'Mr.Piano' Henderson	Sing it again with Joe	18	15-Sep
Doris Day	Love me or leave me	20	15-Sep
Caterina Valente	The breeze and I	5	15-Sep
Nat 'King' Cole	My one sin	17	22-Sep
Ray Burns & The Coronets	That's how a love song was born	14	22-Sep
Tony Bennett	Close your eyes	18	22-Sep
David Whitfield	Ev'rywhere	3	29-Sep
Sammy Davis Jr.	Love me or leave me	8	29-Sep
Slim Whitman	China doll	15	29-Sep
Alma Cogan	The banjo's back in town	17	29-Sep
Al Martino	The man from Laramie	19	29-Sep
Charlie Applewhite & His Orchestra	Blue Star (Theme from The Medic)	20	29-Sep
Stargazers	Close the door	6	06-Oct
Sammy Davis Jr.	That old black magic	16	06-Oct
Lita Roza	Hey there	17	13-Oct
Sammy Davis Jr.	Hey there	19	13-Oct
Jimmy Young	The man from Laramie	1	20-Oct

24

Johnnie Ray	Hernando's hideaway	11	20-Oct
Cyril Stapleton	Blue Star (Theme from The Medic)	2	27-Oct
Doris Day	I'll never stop loving you	17	27-Oct
Central Band Of The Royal Air Force	Dambusters March	18	27-Oct
Mitch Miller	The yellow rose of Texas	2	03-Nov
Alma Cogan	Go on by	16	03-Nov
Ron Goodwin & His Orchestra	Blue Star (Theme from The Medic)	20	03-Nov
Don Lang	Cloudburst	16	10-Nov
Johnston Brothers	Hernando's hideaway	1	17-Nov
Johnnie Ray	Hey there	5	17-Nov
Ruby Murray	I'll come when you call	6	17-Nov
Gary Miller	The yellow rose of Texas	13	17-Nov
Ronnie Hilton	The yellow rose of Texas	15	17-Nov
Frankie Laine	Hummingbird	16	17-Nov
Rosemary Clooney	Hey there	4	24-Nov
Johnnie Ray	Song of the dreamer	10	24-Nov
Bill Haley & His Comets	Rock around the clock	1	01-Dec
Coronets	Twenty tiny fingers	20	01-Dec
Four Aces	Love is a many splendoured thing	2	01-Dec
Winifred Atwell	Let's have a ding dong	3	08-Dec
Stargazers	Twenty tiny fingers	5	15-Dec
Pat Boone	Ain't that a shame	7	15-Dec
Don Charles' Singing Dogs	Oh! Suzanna / medley: Pat-a-cake / Three blind mice / Jingle bells	13	15-Dec
Petula Clark	Suddenly there's a valley	9	15-Dec
Frankie Vaughan	Seventeen	18	15-Dec
Big Ben Banjo Band	Let's get together again	19	15-Dec
Dickie Valentine	Christmas alphabet	1	22-Dec
Harry Secombe	On with the motley	16	22-Dec

David Whitfield & Mantovani	When you lose the one you love	7	22-Dec
Lee Lawrence	Suddenly there's a valley	14	22-Dec
Alma Cogan	Twenty tiny fingers	17	22-Dec
Dickie Valentine	The old pianna rag	20	22-Dec
Max Bygraves	Meet me on the corner	4	29-Dec
Frankie Laine	Hawkeye	7	29-Dec
Jo Stafford	Suddenly there's a valley	12	29-Dec
Anne Shelton	Arrivederci darling	18	29-Dec
Alma Cogan	Never do a tango with an eskimo	13	29-Dec
Boyd Bennett & His Rockets	Seventeen	16	29-Dec
Jimmy Young	Someone on your mind	19	29-Dec
Jimmy Shand Band	Bluebell Polka	20	29-Dec

The events ....

- Cardiff became the official capital of Wales[69]
- A big freeze across Britain resulted in more than 70 roads being blocked with snow, and in some parts of the country rail services were cancelled for several days[70]
- Winterborne St Martin entered the UK Weather Records with the highest 24-hour total rainfall at 279mm – a record which stood until 2009[78]

In the world of sport ......

- Chelsea F.C became First Division Champions for the first time in their history[71]
- Newcastle United won the FA Cup for the sixth time with a 3-1 win over Manchester City at Wembley Stadium[72]
- Stirling Moss became the first English winner of the British Grand Prix at Aintree Motor Racing Circuit[73]
- Duncan Edwards, the 18-year-old Manchester United left-half, became the youngest full England international in a 7-2 win over Scotland at Wembley Stadium[74]

Kanchenjunga
© Dipankar Chetia (2015)
Wikimedia Commons / CC BY-4.0

- Joe Brown and George Band were the first to reach the summit of Kanchenjunga in India, as part of a British team led by Charles Evans[78]

In the world of entertainment.......

The Guinness Book of Records was first published[75]
- The first commercial TV station began broadcasting and the first advertisement was for Gibbs SR toothpaste[76]
- Richard Baker and Kenneth Kendall became the first BBC Television newsreaders to be seen reading the news[81]
Ian Fleming's James Bond novel *Moonraker* was published[78]
J.R.R. Tolkien's *The Return of the King,* the third and final part of *The Lord of the Rings* was published[78]
- The Temperance Seven was founded, with three members[77]

n the world of business.....

The last Cornish engine pumping in the metalliferous mines of Cornwall was shut down at South Crofty[78]
Airfix produced their first scale model aircraft kit, of the Supermarine Spitfire at 1/72 scale[79]
- C. Northcote Parkinson first articulated "Parkinson's Law", the semi-serious adage *Work expands so as to fill the time available for its completion.*[80]

n the world of transport.....

Aircraft carrier HMS *Ark Royal* was commissioned[81]
- Christopher Cockerell patented his design of the hovercraft[78]

HMS Ark Royal
© *Isaac Newton (1976)*
Wikimedia Commons / CC BY-SA-2.5

1956

Welcome to the lighter side of life in Britain in 1956

The music ....

Artist	Title	Highest position this year	W/E date
Dickie Valentine	Christmas alphabet	1	05-Jan
Winifred Atwell	Let's have a ding dong	4	05-Jan
Frankie Laine	Hawkeye	7	05-Jan
Johnston Brothers & The George Chisholm Sour-Note Six	Join in and sing again	9	05-Jan
Mitch Miller	The yellow rose of Texas	11	05-Jan
Jo Stafford	Suddenly there's a valley	13	05-Jan
Johnston Brothers	Hernando's hideaway	15	05-Jan
Anne Shelton	Arrivederci darling	17	05-Jan
Big Ben Banjo Band	Let's get together again	18	05-Jan
Jimmy Shand Band	Bluebell Polka	20	05-Jan
Bill Haley & His Comets	Rock around the clock	1	12-Jan
Max Bygraves	Meet me on the corner	2	12-Jan
Four Aces	Love is a many splendoured thing	3	12-Jan
Stargazers	Twenty tiny fingers	4	12-Jan
Petula Clark	Suddenly there's a valley	7	12-Jan
Alma Cogan	Never do a tango with an eskimo	6	12-Jan
Pat Boone	Ain't that a shame	12	12-Jan
David Whitfield & Mantovani	When you lose the one you love	11	12-Jan
Dickie Valentine	The old pianna rag	15	12-Jan
Jimmy Young	Someone on your mind	13	19-Jan
Bill Haley & His Comets	Rock-a-beatin' boogie	4	19-Jan

28

Edna Savage	Arrivederci darling	19	19-Jan
Don Lang	Cloudburst	20	19-Jan
Bill Hayes	The ballad of Davy Crockett	2	26-Jan
Tennessee Ernie Ford	Sixteen tons	1	26-Jan
Frank Sinatra	Love and marriage	3	26-Jan
Tennessee Ernie Ford	The ballad of Davy Crockett	3	02-Feb
Frankie Laine & The Mellomen	Sixteen tons	10	02-Feb
Billy Vaughan Orchestra	The shifting whispering sands	20	02-Feb
Lonnie Donegan	Rosk Island line	8	09-Feb
Eve Boswell	Pickin' a chicken	9	09-Feb
Gary Miller	Robin Hood	10	09-Feb
Eamonn Andrews	The shifting whispering sands	18	09-Feb
Frankie Vaughan	My boy flat top	20	09-Feb
Fank Sinatra	(Love is) The tender trap	2	16-Feb
Dick James with Stephen James & His Chums	Robin Hood / The ballad of Davy Crockett	14	16-Feb
Malcolm Vaughan	With your love	18	16-Feb
Ronnie Hilton	Young and foolish	17	16-Feb
Dean Martin	Memories are made of this	1	23-Feb
Max Bygraves	The balld of Davy Crockett	20	23-Feb
Lou Busch	Zambesi	2	01-Mar
Nat 'King' Cole	Dreams can tell a lie	10	01-Mar
Johnny Ray	Who's sorry now?	17	01-Mar
Don Cherry	Band of gold	6	08-Mar
Edmund Hockridge	Young and foolish	10	08-Mar
Frank Chacksfield	In old Lisbon	15	08-Mar
Dean Martin	Young and foolish	20	08-Mar
Dave King & The Keynotes	Memories are made of this	5	15-Mar
Dreamweavers	It's almost tomorrow	1	22-Mar
Bill Haley & His Comets	See you later alligator	7	22-Mar
Slim Whitman	Tumbling tumbleweeds	19	22-Mar

Jimmy Young	Chain gang	9	29-Mar
Alfi & Harry	The trouble with Harry	15	29-Mar
Kay Starr	Rock and roll waltz	1	05-Apr
Eddie Calvert	Zambesi	13	05-Apr
Michael Holliday	Nothin' to do	20	05-Apr
Jimmy Parkinson	The great pretender	9	12-Apr
Billy Vaughan Orchestra	Theme from 'The Threepenny Opera'	12	12-Apr
Lita Roza	Jimmy Unknown	15	12-Apr
Cyril Stapleton	The Italian Theme	18	12-Apr
Winifred Atwell	Poor people of Paris	1	19-Apr
Dick Hyman Trio	Theme from 'The Threepenny Opera'	9	19-Apr
Alma Cogan	Willie can	13	19-Apr
Slim Whitman	I'm a fool	16	26-Apr
Anne Shelton	Seven days	20	26-Apr
Johnnie Ray	Ain't misbehavin'	17	03-May
Louis Armstrong	Theme from 'The Threepenny Opera'	8	10-May
Ronnie Hilton	No other love	1	10-May
Dave King & The Keynotes	You can't be true to two	11	10-May
Billy May & His Orchestra	Theme from 'The Man With The Golden Arm'	9	10-May
Hilltoppers	Only you	3	17-May
David Whitfield	My September love	3	24-May
Don Robertson	The happy whistler	8	24-May
Teresa Brewer	A tear fell	2	31-May
Lonnie Donegan	Lost John / Stewball	2	07-Jun
Winifred Atwell & Frank Chacksfield	Port-Au-Prince	18	14-Jun
Three Kayes	Ivory Tower	20	14-Jun
Pat Boone	I'll be home	1	21-Jun
Carl Perkins	Blue suede shoes	10	21-Jun
Elvis Presley	Blue suede shoes	9	21-Jun
Max Bygraves	Out of town	18	21-Jun
Elvis Presley	Heartbreak Hotel	2	28-Jun
Perry Como	Hot diggity	4	28-Jun
Morris Stoloff	Theme from 'Picnic'	7	28-Jun

Michael Holliday	The gal with the yaller shoes	13	28-Jun
Nat 'King' Cole	Too young to go steady	8	05-Jul
Michael Holliday	Hot diggity / The gal with the yaller shoes	14	05-Jul
Bill Haley & His Comets	The Saints rock 'n' roll	5	12-Jul
Lonnie Donegan	Skiffle session – EP (Railroad Bill / Stackalee)	20	12-Jul
Frank Sinatra	Songs for swingin' lovers – EP (You're getting to be a habit with me / You brought a new kind of love to me)	12	12-Jul
Joe 'Fingers' Carr	Portuguese washerwoman	20	12-Jul
Goons	I'm walking backwards for Christmas / Bluebottle blues	4	19-Jul
Johnny Dankworth	Experiments with mice	7	19-Jul
Gogi Grant	The wayward wind	9	19-Jul
Various artists	All star hit parade - EP (Dickie Valentine - Out of town / Joan Regan - My September love / Winifred Atwell - Theme from a Threepenny Opera / Dave King - No other love / Lita Roza - A tear fell	2	19-Jul
Frankie Lymon & The Teenagers	Why do fools fall in love	1	26-Jul
Humphrey Lyttleton Band	Bad penny blues	19	26-Jul
Tex Ritter	The wayward wind	8	09-Aug
Ronnie Hilton	Who are we	6	09-Aug
Mel Torme	Mountain greenery	4	16-Aug
Winifred Atwell	Left bank	14	16-Aug

Doris Day	Whatever will be will be (Que sera sera)	1	16-Aug
Tony Martin	Walk hand in hand	2	16-Aug
Ted Heath & His Music	The faithful Hussar	18	16-Aug
Teresa Brewer	A sweet old-fashioned girl	3	23-Aug
Ronnie Carroll	Walk hand in hand	13	30-Aug
Pat Boone	I almost lost my mind	14	30-Aug
Gene Vincent	Be-bop-a-lula	16	30-Aug
Pat Boone	Long tall Sally	18	30-Aug
Slim Whitman	Serenade	8	06-Sep
Fats Domino	I'm in love again	12	06-Sep
Elvis Presley	I want you, I need you, I love you	14	13-Sep
Chordettes	Born to be with you	8	13-Sep
Ruby Murray	You are my first love	16	13-Sep
Edmund Hockridge	By the fountains of Rome	17	20-Sep
Bill Haley & His Comets	Rockin' through the rye	3	27-Sep
Anne Shelton	Lay down your arms	1	27-Sep
Platters	The great pretender / Only you	5	27-Sep
Goons	Ying tong song / Bloodnock's rock & roll call	3	04-Oct
Lonnie Donegan	Bring a little water Sylvie / Dead or alive	7	04-Oct
Bill Haley & His Comets	Razzle dazzle	13	11-Oct
Frankie Laine	A woman in love	1	25-Oct
Freddie Bell & The Bellboys	Giddy up a ding dong	4	25-Oct
Elvis Presley	Hound dog	2	01-Nov
Perry Como	Glendora	18	01-Nov
Four Aces	A woman in love	19	01-Nov

Tommy Steele	Rock with the caveman	13	08-Nov
Perry Como	More	10	15-Nov
George Melachrino Orchestra	Autumn concerto	18	15-Nov
Platters	My prayer	4	15-Nov
Gene Vincent	Blue jean bop	16	15-Nov
Johnnie Ray	Just walkin' in the rain	1	22-Nov
Jimmy Young	More	4	22-Nov
Nat 'King' Cole	Love me as though there were no tomorrow	11	22-Nov
Jim Lowe & The High Fives	Green door	8	22-Nov
Elvis Presley	Blue moon	9	29-Nov
Mitchell Torok	When Mexico gave up the Rhumba	6	29-Nov
Alma Cogan	In the middle of the house	20	29-Nov
Ronnie Hilton	Two different worlds	13	06-Dec
Frankie Vaughan	Green door	2	13-Dec
Bill Haley & His Comets	Rip it up	4	13-Dec
Vera Lynn	A house with love in it	17	13-Dec
Jimmy Parkinson	In the middle of the house	20	13-Dec
Malcolm Vaughan	St.Therese of the Roses	3	20-Dec
Winifred Atwell	Make it a party	9	27-Dec
Eddie Fisher	Cindy oh Cindy	5	27-Dec
Bing Crosby & Grace Kelly	True love	7	27-Dec
Guy Mitchell	Singing the blues	4	27-Dec
Elvis Presley	Love me tender	14	27-Dec
Dickie Valentine	Christmas island	12	27-Dec
Tony Brent	Cindy oh Cindy	16	27-Dec
Tommy Steele	Singing the blues	19	27-Dec
Pat Boone	Friendly persuasion	20	27-Dec

The events ....

• The Gower Peninsula of Wales became the first area in the British Isles to be designated an Area of Outstanding Natural Beauty[82]

- In his budget speech, Chancellor of the Exchequer Harold Macmillan announced the launch of Premium Bonds that would go on sale from November and have a £1,000 prize available from June 1957[83],[84],[85]
- Parliament passed the Clean Air Act in response to the Great Smog of 1952[86]
- Guy Mollet visited London and proposed a merger of France and the United Kingdom however, the idea was rejected by Anthony Eden[87]

In the world of sport ……

- Manchester United, with an average team age of 24, won the First Division Football League title[88]
- Manchester City won the FA Cup with a 3-1 defeat of Birmingham City at Wembley Stadium[89]
- Great Britain and Northern Ireland competed at the Winter Olympics in Italy but did not win any medals[89]
- Great Britain and Northern Ireland competed at the Summer Olympics in Melbourne, Australia and won 6 gold, 7 silver and 11 bronze medals[89]
- Manchester United became the first English team to compete in the European Cup when they played the first leg of the preliminary round in Belgium and beat R.S.C. Anderlecht 2-0[89]
- Manchester United qualified for the first round of the European Cup with a 10-0 win of R.S.C. Anderlecht at Maine Road in the second leg[89]

In the world of entertainment…….

- Granada Television launched with a base in Manchester[96]
- The long-running TV programme *What the Papers Say* was aired for the first time[96]
- Ian Fleming's James Bond novel *Diamonds Are Forever* was published[89]
- Dodie Smith's children's novel *The Hundred and One Dalmatians* was published[89]
- The musical film *A Touch Of The Sun* was released starring Frankie Howerd, Ruby Murray and Dennis Price[90]

In the world of business…..

- Corgi toy metal cars were first introduced by Mettoy[91]
- The TAT-1 transatlantic telephone cable between the UK and North America was inaugurated[96]
- The world's first commercial nuclear power station was opened in Calder Hall, UK[92]
- Tesco opened its first self-service stores in St. Albansand Maldon[93],[94]
- The first Berni Inn steakhouse opened in Bristol[95]

PG Tips launched its long-running ITV advertising campaign using a chimpanzee's tea party[89]

Corgi model car (2007)
Wikimedia Commons /
Public Domain

n the world of education.....

The first Welsh-medium secondary school in Wales was opened at Ysgol Glan Clwyd, Rhyl[89]

n the world of transport.....

Double yellow lines were first introduced in Slough, Berkshire to prohibit parking[96]

The RAF retired its last Lancaster bomber[96]

Petrol rationing was introduced as a result of the petrol blockades from the Middle East dues to the Suez Crisis[97]

1957

Welcome to the lighter side of life in Britain in 1957

The music ......

Artist	Title	Highest position this year	W/E date
Vera Lynn	A house with love in it	18	03-Jan
Dickie Valentine	Christmas island	8	03-Jan
Tony Brent	Cindy oh Cindy	20	03-Jan
Frankie Vaughan	Green door	3	03-Jan
Johnnie Ray	Just walkin' in the rain	1	03-Jan
Elvis Presley	Love me tender	11	03-Jan
Winifred Atwell	Make it a party	7	03-Jan
Jimmy Young	More	13	03-Jan
Platters	My prayer	10	03-Jan
Bill Haley & His Comets	Rip it up	9	03-Jan
Malcolm Vaughan	St.Therese of the Roses	3	03-Jan
Frankie Laine	A woman in love	10	10-Jan
Eddie Fisher	Cindy oh Cindy	5	10-Jan
Elvis Presley	Hound dog	8	10-Jan
Frankie Laine	Moonlight gambler	13	10-Jan
Bill Haley & His Comets	Rockin' through the rye	19	10-Jan
Guy Mitchell	Singing the blues	1	10-Jan
Ronnie Hilton	Two different worlds	18	10-Jan
Mitchell Torok	When Mexico gave up the Rhumba	12	10-Jan
Elvis Presley	Blue moon	17	17-Jan
Pat Boone	I'll be home	19	17-Jan
Tommy Steele	Singing the blues	1	17-Jan
Gary Miller	Garden of Eden	14	24-Jan
Alma Cogan	You, me and us	18	24-Jan
Pat Boone	Friendly persuasion	3	31-Jan
Frankie Vaughan	Garden of Eden	1	31-Jan
Dick James	Garden of Eden	18	31-Jan
Bill Haley & His Comets	Rock this joint	20	07-Feb

Fats Domino	Blueberry Hill	6	14-Feb
Vipers Skiffle Group	Don't you rock me Daddy-O	10	14-Feb
Bing Crosby & Grace Kelly	True love	4	14-Feb
Bill Haley & His Comets	Don't knock the rock	7	21-Feb
Lonnie Donegan	Don't you rock me Daddy-O	4	21-Feb
Jerry Lewis	Rock-a-bye your baby	12	21-Feb
Tommy Steele	Knee deep in the blues	15	28-Feb
Tab Hunter	Young love	1	28-Feb
David Whitfield	The adoration waltz	9	07-Mar
Sonny James	Young love	11	07-Mar
Pat Boone	Don't forbid me	2	14-Mar
Guy Mitchell	Knee deep in the blues	3	14-Mar
Tarriers	The banana boat song	15	21-Mar
Norman Wisdom	The wisdom of a fool	13	28-Mar
Little Richard	Long tall Sally	3	04-Apr
Shirley Bassey	The banana boat song	8	04-Apr
Platters	The great pretender / Only you	18	04-Apr
Ronnie Carroll	The wisdom of a fool	20	04-Apr
Hilltoppers	Marianne	20	11-Apr
Little Richard	She's got it	15	11-Apr
Vipers Skiffle Group	Cumberland gap	10	18-Apr
Lonnie Donegan	Cumberland gap	1	18-Apr
Max Bygraves	Heart	14	18-Apr
Harry Belafonte	The banana boat song	2	18-Apr
Little Richard	The girl can't help it	9	18-Apr
Frankie Lymon & The Teenagers	I'm not a juvenile delinquent	12	25-Apr
Fats Domino	I'm walkin'	19	25-Apr
Johnnie Ray	Look homeward angel	7	25-Apr
Tab Hunter	99 ways	5	09-May
Frankie Lymon & The Teenagers	Baby baby	4	09-May
Johnnie Ray	You don't owe me a thing / Look homeward angel	7	09-May
Pat Boone	Why baby why	17	16-May
Frankie Laine	Love is a golden ring	19	23-May

Guy Mitchell	Rock-a-billy	1	23-May
Andy Williams	Butterfly	1	30-May
Charlie Gracie	Butterfly	12	30-May
Slim Whitman	I'll take you home again, Kathleen	7	30-May
Rosemary Clooney	Mangos	17	30-May
Malcolm Vaughan	Chapel of the roses	13	06-Jun
Chas McDevitt & Nancy Whiskey	Freight train	5	06-Jun
Platters	I'm sorry	18	06-Jun
Elvis Presley	Too much	6	06-Jun
Gracie Fields	Around the world	8	13-Jun
Mantovani & His Orchestra	Around the world	20	13-Jun
Peggy Lee	Mr.Wonderful	5	13-Jun
Johnnie Ray	Yes tonight, Josephine	1	13-Jun
Nat 'King' Cole	When I fall in love	2	20-Jun
Terry Dene	A white sport coat and a pink carnation	18	27-Jun
Bing Crosby	Around the world	5	27-Jun
King Brothers	A white sport coat and a pink carnation	6	04-Jul
Lonnie Donegan	Gamblin' man / Puttin' on the style	1	04-Jul
Ronnie Hilton	Around the world	4	11-Jul
Vera Lynn	Travellin' home	20	11-Jul
Elvis Presley	All shook up	1	18-Jul
Andy Williams	I like your kind of love	16	18-Jul
Diamonds	Little darlin'	3	18-Jul
Tommy Steele	Butterfingers	8	25-Jul
Elvis Presley	(Let me be your) Teddy bear	3	08-Aug
Little Richard	Lucille	10	08-Aug
Russ Hamilton	We will make love	2	08-Aug
Pat Boone	Love letters in the sand	2	22-Aug
Sal Mineo	Start movin' (in my direction)	15	22-Aug
Harry Belafonte	Island in the sun	3	29-Aug

Various Artists	All star hit parade volume 2 - EP (Johnston Brothers - Around the world / Billy Cotton - Puttin' on the style / Jimmy Young - When I fall in love / Max Bygraves - A white sport coat / Beverley Sisters - Freight train / Tommy Steele - Butterfly)	15	29-Aug
Everly Brothers	Bye bye love	6	05-Sep
Tony Brent	Dark moon	17	05-Sep
Paul Anka	Diana	1	05-Sep
Charlie Gracie	Fabulous	8	05-Sep
Tommy Steele	Shiralee	11	12-Sep
Johnny Duncan	Last train to San Fernando	2	19-Sep
Elvis Presley	Paralysed	8	19-Sep
Tommy Steele	Water water / A handful of songs	5	19-Sep
King Brothers	In the middle of an island	19	26-Sep
Johnnie Ray	Build your love	17	03-Oct
Little Richard	Jenny Jenny	11	03-Oct
Harry Belafonte & Millard Thomas	Scarlet ribbons	18	03-Oct
Billy Ward & The Dominoes	Stardust	13	03-Oct
Petula Clark	With all my heart	4	03-Oct
Peter Sellers	Any old iron	17	17-Oct
Guy Mitchell	Call Rosie on the phone	17	24-Oct
Russ Hamilton	Wedding ring	20	24-Oct
Elvis Presley	Party	2	31-Oct
Charlie Gracie	I love you so much it hurts / Wanderin' eyes	6	31-Oct
Frankie Vaughan	Man on fire / Wanderin' eyes	6	07-Nov
Debbie Reynolds	Tammy	2	07-Nov

Pat Boone	Remember you're mine / There's a gold mine in the sky	5	07-Nov
Buddy Holly & The Crickets	That'll be the day	1	07-Nov
Jerry Lee Lewis	Whole lotta shakin' goin' on	8	07-Nov
Elvis Presley	Got a lot o' livin' to do	17	14-Nov
Frankie Vaughan & The Kaye Sisters	Gotta have something in the bank Frank	8	14-Nov
Lonnie Donegan	My Dixie darling	10	14-Nov
Elvis Presley	Trying to get to you	16	21-Nov
Elvis Presley	Lawdy Miss Clawdy	15	28-Nov
Harry Belafonte	Mary's boy child	1	28-Nov
Shepherd Sisters	Alone	14	05-Dec
Jim Dale	Be my girl	2	05-Dec
Southlanders	Alone	18	12-Dec
Laurie London	He's got the whole world in his hands	12	12-Dec
Petula Clark	Alone	8	19-Dec
Paul Anka	I love you baby	3	19-Dec
Malcolm Vaughan	My special angel	5	19-Dec
Elvis Presley	Santa bring my baby back to me	7	19-Dec
Everly Brothers	Wake up little Susie	2	19-Dec
Pat Boone	April love	16	26-Dec
Frank Sinatra	Chicago / All the way	7	26-Dec
Jerry Lee Lewis	Great balls of fire	12	26-Dec
Lonnie Donegan	Jack O' Diamonds	19	26-Dec
Jimmie Rodgers	Kisses sweeter than wine	20	26-Dec
Winifred Atwell	Let's have a ball	8	26-Dec
Johnny Otis Show	Ma, he's making eyes at me	2	26-Dec
Jackie Wilson	Reet petite	8	26-Dec

The events.........

- The first Premium Bond winners were selected by the computer ERNIE[105]
- Norwich City Council became the first British local authority to install a computer (an Elliott 405)[98]

40

Wales got its own minister of state in the Westminster government for the first time[103]

n the world of sport ……

Manchester United retained the Football League First Division title with a 4-0 win over Sunderland[99]
Aston Villa won the FA Cup with a 2-1 defeat of Manchester United at Wembley Stadium[100]
Stirling Moss won the first Motor Racing world championship for a British car in a Vanwall VW5 at Aintree[101]
Tony Lock became the last bowler to reach 200 wickets in a first-class season[102]

Vanwall VW5
© *Terry Whalebone (1957) / Wikimedia Commons / CC BY-2.0*

n the world of entertainment…….

The 'Toddlers Truce', an arrangement where there were no television broadcasts between 6pm and 7pm to allow parents to put their children to bed, was abolished.[103]
The BBC broadcasted a spoof documentary showing spaghetti being harvested in Switzerland, believed to be the first April Fool's Day joke on television[104]
The first broadcast of *'The Sky At Night'* took place with Patrick Moore hosting– and

The Cavern Club
© *Flickr (2009) / Wikimedia Commons / CC BY-SA-2.0 Generic*

continued with the same presenter until his death in 2012[103]
'Andy Capp' first appeared in the Northern edition of the Daily Mirror[103]
The Cavern Club opened in Liverpool[105]
John Lennon and Paul McCartney first met at the St.Peter's Church garden fete[106]
Central Scotland's independent channel Scottish Television went on air, the first 7-day-a-week ITV franchise to do so[103]
The Royal Christmas message was broadcast on television with the Queen on camera for the first time[105]
Ian Fleming's James Bond novel *From Russia with Love* was published[103]
Alistair MacLean's wartime adventure novel *The Guns of Navarone* was published[103]

41

- Patricia Bredin represented the UK at the 2nd Eurovision Song Contest in Frankfurt, finishing in 7th place[106]

In the world of business.....

- 'Which?' Magazine was first published[103]

In the world of transport.....

- Petrol rationing as a result of the Suez Crisis came to an end[107]

1958

Welcome to the lighter side of life in Britain in 1958

The music ....

Artist	Title	Highest position this year	W/E date
Petula Clark	Alone	9	02-Jan
Jim Dale	Be my girl	11	02-Jan
Lonnie Donegan	Jack O' Diamonds	14	02-Jan
Winifred Atwell	Let's have a ball	4	02-Jan
Johnny Otis Show	Ma, he's making eyes at me	2	02-Jan
Harry Belafonte	Mary's boy child	1	02-Jan
Malcolm Vaughan	My special angel	3	02-Jan
Pat Boone	Remember you're mine / There's a goldmine in the sky	18	02-Jan
Elvis Presley	Santa bring my baby back to me	20	02-Jan
Southlanders	Alone	17	09-Jan
Paul Anka	Diana	10	09-Jan
Elvis Presley	Party	12	09-Jan
Jackie Wilson	Reet petite	6	09-Jan
Everly Brothers	Wake up little Susie	2	09-Jan
Jerry Lee Lewis	Great balls of fire	1	16-Jan
Laurie London	He's got the whole world in his hands	17	16-Jan
Paul Anka	I love you baby	6	16-Jan
Frank Sinatra	All the way / Chicago	3	23-Jan
Frankie Vaughan	Kisses sweeter than wine	8	23-Jan
Jimmie Rodgers	Kisses sweeter than wine	7	23-Jan
Buddy Holly & The Crickets	Peggy Sue	6	23-Jan
Elvis Presley	Jailhouse rock	1	30-Jan
Dave King	The story of my life	20	30-Jan

Buddy Holly & The Crickets	Oh boy!	3	06-Feb
Gary Miller	The story of my life	14	06-Feb
Johnny Otis Show	Bye bye baby	20	13-Feb
Pat Boone	April love	7	20-Feb
Elvis Presley	Jailhouse rock - EP - Jailhouse rock / Young and beautiful / I want to be free / Don't leave me now / (You're so square) Baby I don't care	18	20-Feb
Michael Holliday	The story of my life	1	20-Feb
Bill Justis	Raunchy	11	27-Feb
Ken Mackintosh	Raunchy	19	27-Feb
McGuire Sisters	Sugartime	14	27-Feb
Larry Williams	Bony Moronie	11	06-Mar
Marion Ryan	Love me forever	5	06-Mar
Perry Como	Magic moments	1	06-Mar
Frank Sinatra	Witchcraft	12	06-Mar
Frankie Vaughan	Can't get along without you / We are not alone	11	13-Mar
Paul Anka	You are my destiny	6	13-Mar
Petula Clark	Baby lover	12	20-Mar
Buddy Holly & The Crickets	Listen to me	16	20-Mar
Danny & The Juniors	At the hop	3	27-Mar
Perry Como	Catch a falling star	9	27-Mar
Little Richard	Good golly Miss Molly	8	27-Mar
Elvis Presley	Don't	2	03-Apr
Alma Cogan	Sugartime	16	03-Apr
Eddie Calvert	Mandy (La Panse)	9	10-Apr
Tommy Steele	Nairobi	3	10-Apr
Jackie Dennis	La dee dah	4	17-Apr
Fats Domino	The big beat	20	17-Apr
Buddy Holly & The Crickets	Maybe baby	4	24-Apr
Jimmie Rodgers	Oh-oh I'm falling in love again	18	24-Apr
Ted Heath & His Music	Swingin' shepherd blues	3	24-Apr

44

Tommy Steele	Happy guitar	20	01-May
Pat Boone	It's too soon to know	7	01-May
Champs	Tequila	5	01-May
Malcolm Vaughan & The Michael Sammes Singers	To be loved	14	01-May
Marvin Rainwater	Whole lotta woman	1	01-May
Jerry Lee Lewis	Breathless	8	08-May
Chordettes	Lollipop	6	15-May
Chuck Berry	Sweet little sixteen	16	15-May
Tony Brent	The clouds will soon roll by	20	15-May
Pat Boone	A wonderful time up there	2	22-May
Connie Francis	Who's sorry now	1	22-May
Robert Earl	I may never pass this way again	14	29-May
Ella Fitzgerald	Swingin' shepherd blues	15	29-May
Elias & His Zig Zag Jive Flutes	Tom Hark	2	29-May
Elvis Presley	Wear my ring around your neck	3	29-May
Perry Como	Kewpie doll	9	05-Jun
Mudlarks	Lollipop	2	05-Jun
Terry Dene	Stairway of love	16	05-Jun
Lonnie Donegan	The Grand Coolie dam	6	05-Jun
David Seville	Witch doctor	11	05-Jun
Frankie Vaughan	Kewpie doll	10	12-Jun
Perry Como	I may never pass this way again	15	19-Jun
Michael Holliday	Stairway of love	3	19-Jun
Don Lang & His Frantic Five	Witch doctor	5	19-Jun
Marvin Rainwater	I dig you baby	19	26-Jun
Vic Damone	On the street where you live	1	03-Jul
Original Cast Of The Army Game	Theme from 'The Army Game'	5	03-Jul
Everly Brothers	All I have to do is dream / Claudette	1	10-Jul

45

Mudlarks	Book of love	8	10-Jul
Max Bygraves	Tulips from Amsterdam / You need hands	3	10-Jul
Sheb Wooley	Purple people eater	12	17-Jul
Platters	Twilight time	3	17-Jul
Four Preps	Big man	2	24-Jul
David Whitfield	On the street where you live	16	24-Jul
Lonnie Donegan	Sally don't grieve / Betty Betty Betty	11	24-Jul
Pat Boone	Sugar moon	6	24-Jul
Tommy Steele	The only man on the island	16	24-Jul
Doris Day	A very precious love	16	07-Aug
Elvis Presley	Hard headed woman	2	07-Aug
Buddy Holly & The Crickets	Rave on	5	07-Aug
Julius La Rosa	Torero	15	07-Aug
Connie Francis	I'm sorry I made you cry	11	14-Aug
Bobby Helms	Jacqueline	20	14-Aug
Joe 'Mr.Piano' Henderson	Trudie	14	21-Aug
Buddy Holly & The Crickets	Think it over	11	28-Aug
Kalin Twins	When	1	28-Aug
Marty Wilde	Endless sleep	4	04-Sep
Harry Belafonte	Little Bernadette	16	04-Sep
Bobby Darin	Splish splash	18	04-Sep
Buddy Holly & The Crickets	Early in the morning	17	11-Sep
Perez Prado	Patricia	8	11-Sep
Dean Martin	Return to me	2	11-Sep
Coasters	Yakety Yak	12	11-Sep
Duane Eddy	Rebel rouser	19	18-Sep
Charlie Drake	Splish splash	7	18-Sep
Domenico Modugno	Volare	10	18-Sep
Tony Brent	Girl of my dreams	16	25-Sep
Peggy Lee	Fever	5	02-Oct
Connie Francis	Stupid cupid / Carolina moon	1	02-Oct

Dean Martin	Volare	2	02-Oct
Pat Boone	If dreams came true	16	09-Oct
Bernard Bresslaw	Mad passionate love	6	09-Oct
Ricky Nelson	Poor little fool	4	09-Oct
Marino Marini Quartet	Volare	13	16-Oct
Poni-Tails	Born too late	5	23-Oct
Elvis Presley	King Creole	2	23-Oct
Jodie Sands	Someday (you'll want me to want you)	14	23-Oct
Marino Marini Quartet	Come prima	2	30-Oct
Cliff Richard & The Drifters	Move it	2	30-Oct
Olympics	Western movies	12	06-Nov
Tommy Edwards	It's all in the game	1	13-Nov
Perry Como	Moon talk	17	13-Nov
Everly Brothers	Bird dog	2	20-Nov
Jack Scott	My true love	9	20-Nov
Johnny Mathis	A certain smile	4	27-Nov
Connie Francis	I'll get by	19	27-Nov
Malcolm Vaughan & The Michael Sammes Singers	More than ever (Come prima)	5	27-Nov
Connie Francis	Fallin'	20	04-Dec
Lord Rockingham's XI	Hoots mon	1	04-Dec
Eddie Cochran	Summertime blues	18	04-Dec
Lonnie Donegan	Tom Dooley	3	11-Dec
Cliff Richard & The Drifters	High class baby	7	18-Dec
Perry Como	Mandolins in the moonlight	16	18-Dec
Ruby Murray	Real love	18	18-Dec
Ricky Nelson	Someday	9	18-Dec
Kingston Trio	Tom Dooley	6	18-Dec
Tommy Steele	Come on let's go	12	25-Dec
Conway Twitty	It's only make believe	1	25-Dec
Perry Como	Love makes the world go round	7	25-Dec
Russ Conway	More party pops	16	25-Dec
Tommy Dorsey Orchestra feat. Warren Covington	Tea for two cha-cha	4	25-Dec
Jane Morgan	The day the rains came	11	25-Dec

Harry Belafonte	The son of Mary	18	25-Dec

The events........

- The London Planetarium first opened in Britain[108]
- A British team led by Sir Vivian Fuchs completed the first crossing of the Antarctic using Sno-Cat caterpillar tractors and dogsled teams in 99 days[108]
- The Duke of Edinburgh's award was presented for the first time[108]
- Ian Fraser, Baron Fraser of Lonsdale and Barbara Wootton, Baroness Wootton of Abinger, became the first life peers[109]
- The first service took place by a Royal National Lifeboat Institution *Oakley*-class self-righting life-boat, RNLB *J.G.Graves of Sheffield* (ON 942) at Scarborough[110]

THE DUKE
OF EDINBURGH'S
AWARD

Duke of Edinburgh Award (1956) Wikimedia Commons / Public Domain

In the world of sport ......

- Bolton Wanderers won the FA Cup with a 2-0 win over Manchester United at Wembley Stadium[111]
- BBC Television's Grandstand was broadcast for the first time[108]
- Donald Campbell set the world water speed record at 248.62 mph[108]
- The British Empire and Commonwealth Games were held in Cardiff[111]

In the world of entertainment.......

- TWW, the ITV franchise for South Wales and the West of England went on the air[111]
- The musical *'My Fair Lady'* opened in London's West End starring Rex Harrison and Audrey Hepburn[108]
- Southern Television, the ITV franchise for South Central and South East England went on the air[111]
- BBC Television's *'Blue Peter'* was broadcast for the first time[108]
- The State Opening of Parliament was broadcast on television for the first time[108]
- The children's story *'A Bear Called Paddington'* was first published[111]
- Cleo Laine and Johnny Dankworth were married[112]
- H.E. Bates' novel *The Darling Buds of May* was published[111]

Audrey Hepburn Credit: Paramount (1956) / Wikimedia Commons / Public Domain

The UK decided not to compete in the third annual Eurovision Song Contest, after coming 7th in the previous year[112]

In the world of business.....

The world's first computer exhibition was held at Earl's Court in London[111]
The first Subscriber Trunk Dialling (STD) call was made by the Queen from Bristol to the Lord Provost in Edinburgh[113]
The first boutique in London's Carnaby Street, His Clothes, was opened[114]

In the world of transport.....

Work began on the M1, Britain's first full length motorway between London and the Warwickshire/Northamptonshire border[111]
BOAC used its new De Havilland Comet 4 to become the first airline to fly jet passenger services across the Atlantic[111]
The Queen officially re-opened Gatwick Airport, which had been expanded at a cost of more than £7 million[111]
The first parking meters were installed in Britain[108]
The Preston Bypass, Britain's first motorway, was opened by Prime Minister Harold Macmillan[115]
The Austin FX4 London taxi first went on sale and would remain in production until 1997[111]

Paddington Bear
© Lonpicman (2005) /
Wikimedia Commons /
CC BY-SA-3.0 Unported

Austin FX4 London Taxi
© Munbill (2009) /
Wikimedia Commons / CC BY-SA 3.0

The Short SC.1 experimental VTOL aircraft made its first free vertical flight[111]

Short SC.1
© Ruth AS (1958) / Wikimedia Commons /
CC BY 3.0

1959

Welcome to the lighter side of life in Britain in 1959

The music ……

Artist	Title	Highest position this year	W/E date
Johnny Mathis	A certain smile	14	01-Jan
Everly Brothers	Bird dog	19	01-Jan
Tommy Steele	Come on let's go	10	01-Jan
Marino Marini Quartet	Come prima	15	01-Jan
Lord Rockingham's XI	Hoots mon	2	01-Jan
Tommy Edwards	It's all in the game	4	01-Jan
Conway Twitty	It's only make believe	1	01-Jan
Harry Belafonte	Mary's boy child	12	01-Jan
Malcolm Vaughan & The Michael Sammes Singers	More than ever (Coma prima)	11	01-Jan
Ruby Murray	Real love	20	01-Jan
Lonnie Donegan	Tom Dooley	3	01-Jan
Johnny Mathis	Winter wonderland	17	01-Jan
Russ Conway	More party pops	10	08-Jan
Ricky Nelson	Someday	12	08-Jan
Tommy Dorsey Orchestra feat. Warren Covington	Tea for two cha-cha	3	08-Jan
Kingston Trio	Tom Dooley	5	08-Jan
Max Bygraves	(I love to play) My ukelele	19	15-Jan
Cliff Richard & The Drifters	High class baby	8	15-Jan
Perry Como	Love makes the world go round	6	15-Jan
Perry Como	Mandolins in the moonlight	13	15-Jan
Jimmie Rodgers	Woman from Liberia	18	15-Jan
Connie Francis	You always hurt the one you love	13	22-Jan

Little Richard	Baby face	2	29-Jan
Jane Morgan	The day the rains came	1	29-Jan
Al Saxon	You're the top cha cha	17	29-Jan
Big Bopper	Chantilly lace	12	05-Feb
Elvis Presley	One night / I got stung	1	05-Feb
Teddy Bears	To know him is to love him	2	05-Feb
Shirley Bassey	Kiss me, honey honey, kiss me	3	12-Feb
Everly Brothers	Problems	6	12-Feb
Ronnie Hilton & The Mike Sammes Singers	The world outside	18	12-Feb
Paul Anka	(All of a sudden) My heart sings	10	19-Feb
Jerry Lee Lewis	High school confidential	12	19-Feb
Rosemary June	I'll be with you in apple blossom time	14	19-Feb
Four Aces	The world outside	18	19-Feb
Lord Rockingham's XI	Wee Tom	16	19-Feb
Shirley Bassey	As I love you	1	26-Feb
Harry Simeone Chorale	Little drummer boy	13	26-Feb
Lonnie Donegan	Does your chewing gum lose its flavour (on the bedpost overnight)	3	05-Mar
Michael Flanders	Little drummer boy	20	05-Mar
Slim Dusty	A pub with no beer	3	12-Mar
Beverley Sisters	Little drummer boy	6	19-Mar
Robert Earl	The wonderful secret of love	17	19-Mar
Billy Eckstine	Gigi	8	26-Mar
Pat Boone	I'll remember tonight	18	26-Mar
Reg Owen	Manhattan spiritual	20	26-Mar
Platters	Smoke gets in your eyes	1	26-Mar
Lloyd Price	Stagger Lee	7	26-Mar
Connie Francis	My happiness	4	02-Apr
Russ Conway	Side saddle	1	02-Apr
Pearl Carr & Teddy Johnson	Sing little birdie	12	09-Apr

Perry Como	Tomboy	10	09-Apr
Malcolm Vaughan	Wait for me / Willingly	13	09-Apr
Little Richard	By the light of the silvery moon	17	16-Apr
Billy Fury	Maybe tomorrow	18	16-Apr
Eddie Cochran	C'mon everybody	6	23-Apr
Chris Barber's Jazz Band	Petite Fleur	3	23-Apr
Coasters	Charlie Brown	6	30-Apr
Frank Sinatra	French Foreign Legion	18	30-Apr
Buddy Holly & The Crickets	It doesn't matter anymore	1	30-Apr
Dickie Valentine	Venus	20	07-May
Elvis Presley	A fool such as I / I need your love tonight	1	21-May
Fleetwoods	Come softly to me	6	21-May
Marty Wilde	Donna	3	21-May
Lonnie Donegan	Fort Worth jail	14	21-May
Anthony Newley	Idle on parade - EP (I've waited so long / Idle rock-a-boogie / Idle on parade / Sat'day night rock-a-boogie)	13	21-May
Frankie Avalon	Venus	16	21-May
Frankie Vaughan & The Kaye Sisters	Come softly to me	9	28-May
Ricky Nelson	It's late	3	28-May
Cliff Richard & The Drifters	Mean streak	10	28-May
Lloyd Price	Where were you (on our wedding day)?	15	28-May
Fats Domino	Margie	18	04-Jun
McGuire Sisters	May you always	15	04-Jun
Bert Weedon	Guitar boogie shuffle	10	11-Jun
Anthony Newley	I've waited so long	3	11-Jun
Neil Sedaka	I go ape	9	18-Jun
Ruby Wright	Three stars	19	18-Jun
Joan Regan	May you always	9	25-Jun
Ricky Nelson	Never be anyone else but you	14	25-Jun
Russ Conway	Roulette	1	25-Jun

Johnny Horton	Battle of New Orleans	16	09-Jul
Bobby Darin	Dream lover	1	09-Jul
Pat Boone	For a penny	19	09-Jul
Anthony Newley	Personality	6	09-Jul
Marty Wilde	A teenager in love	2	16-Jul
Ruby Murray	Goodbye Jimmy, goodbye	10	16-Jul
Lloyd Price	Personality	9	16-Jul
Duane Eddy	Peter Gunn	6	16-Jul
Everly Brothers	Poor Jenny	14	16-Jul
Everly Brothers	Take a message to Mary	20	16-Jul
Lonnie Donegan	Battle of New Orleans	2	30-Jul
Craig Douglas	A teenager in love	13	06-Aug
Cliff Richard & The Drifters	Living doll	1	06-Aug
Duane Eddy	Yep!	17	06-Aug
Elvis Presley	A big hunk 'o love	4	13-Aug
David Seville & The Chipmunks	Ragtime Cowboy Joe	11	20-Aug
Pat Boone	Twixt twelve and twenty	18	20-Aug
Connie Francis	Lipstick on your collar	3	27-Aug
Perry Como	I know	13	27-Aug
Paul Anka	Lonely boy	3	03-Sep
Freddy Cannon	Tallahassee Lassie	17	03-Sep
Tommy Steele	Tallahassee Lassie	16	03-Sep
Ricky Nelson	Sweeter than you	19	10-Sep
Frankie Vaughan	The heart of a man	5	10-Sep
Russ Conway	China tea	5	17-Sep
Craig Douglas	Only sixteen	1	17-Sep
Lonnie Donegan	Sal's got a sugar lip	13	17-Sep
Johnny Mathis	Someone	6	17-Sep
Duane Eddy	Forty miles of bad road	11	24-Sep
Conway Twitty	Mona Lisa	5	01-Oct
Connie Francis	Plenty good lovin'	18	01-Oct
Ricky Nelson	Just a little too much	11	08-Oct
Buddy Holly & The Crickets	Peggy Sue got married	13	08-Oct
Jerry Keller	Here comes summer	1	15-Oct
Bobby Darin	Mack the Knife	1	22-Oct

Cliff Richard & The Shadows	Dynamite	16	22-Oct
Browns	The three bells	6	22-Oct
Everly Brothers	(Til) I kissed you	2	29-Oct
Sarah Vaughan	Broken-hearted melody	7	05-Nov
Marty Wilde	Sea of love	3	05-Nov
Cliff Richard & The Shadows	Travellin' light	1	05-Nov
Frank Sinatra	High hopes	6	12-Nov
Fats Domino	I want to walk you home	14	12-Nov
David MacBeth	Mr.Blue	18	12-Nov
Floyd Robinson	Makin' love	9	19-Nov
Mike Preston	Mr.Blue	12	19-Nov
Johnny & The Hurricanes	Red River rock	3	19-Nov
Dickie Valentine	One more sunrise	14	26-Nov
Paul Anka	Put your head on my shoulder	7	26-Nov
Coasters	Poison Ivy	15	10-Dec
Lonnie Donegan	San Miguel	19	10-Dec
Adam Faith	What do you want?	1	10-Dec
Connie Francis	Among my souvenirs	12	17-Dec
Marty Wilde	Bad boy	18	17-Dec
Beverley Sisters	Little donkey	14	17-Dec
Sandy Nelson	Teen beat	9	17-Dec
Wink Martindale	Deck of cards	18	24-Dec
Neil Sedaka	Oh Carol	3	24-Dec
Winifred Atwell	Piano party	10	24-Dec
Frankie Laine	Rawhide	8	24-Dec
Avons	Seven little girls (sitting in the back seat)	4	24-Dec
Emile Ford & The Checkmates	What do you want to make those eyes at me for?	1	24-Dec
Fats Domino	Be my guest	17	31-Dec
Max Bygraves	Jingle bell rock	11	31-Dec
Tommy Steele	Little white bull	10	31-Dec
Russ Conway	More and more party pops	5	31-Dec

Russ Conway	Snow coach	7	31-Dec
Duane Eddy	Some kind-a-earthquake	15	31-Dec
Elmer Bernstein	Staccato's theme	6	31-Dec

The events ....

UK Postcodes were introduced for the first time, as an experiment, in the city of Norwich[116]

Dense fog brought chaos to Britain[117]

The official name of the administrative county of Hampshire was changed from 'County of Southampton' to 'County of Hampshire'.[119]

British Empire Day was changed to Commonwealth Day[119]

In the world of sport ......

Nottingham Forest beat Luton Town 2-1 in the FA Cup final at Wembley Stadium[119]

In the world of entertainment........

'Juke Box Jury' was first shown on BBC Television and hosted by David Jacobs with a panel of Pete Murray, Alma Cogan, Gary Miller and Susan Stranks[118]

'Ronnie Scott's' jazz club opened in Soho, London[119]

Bush TR-82 Halogen Highlight
Credit: AurigaM36 (2006) / Wikimedia Commons / Public Domain

Ivor the Engine
© Fidodogsimmons2 at en.Wikipedia (2007) / Wikimedia Commons / CC BY-SA 3.0 Unported

Associated-Rediffusion first aired the children's television series *Ivor the Engine*'[119]

The iconic Bush TR82 transistor radio was launched[119]

Ian Fleming's James Bond novel 'Goldfinger' was published[119]

Tyne Tees Television, the ITV franchise for North East England, went on the air[119]

- The Mermaid Theatre opened in the City of London[119]
- Keith Waterhouse's novel *Billy Liar* was published[119]

In the world of business.....

- Barclays became the first bank to install a computer[120]
- United Dairies merged with Cow & Gate Ltd (of Guildford) to form Unigate Dairies[121]
- House of Fraser won the bidding war for Harrods in a £37 million deal[122]
- Britain became a founder member of the European Free Trade Association[119]
- Tube Investments, allied with Reynolds Metals of the United States and advised by Siegmund Warburg of S.G. Warburg & Co, concluded the first hostile takeover of a public company in the UK[123]

In the world of transport.....

- Christopher Cockerell's invention of the hovercraft was officially launched[124]
- The first Mini went on sale[125]
- The first section of the M1 motorway was opened between Watford and Rugby[125]

Austin Mini
© *DeFacto (2007) / Wikimedia Commons /*
CC BY-SA 2.5

Routemaster bus
© *Chris Sampson (2004) / Wikimedia*
Commons / CC BY-SA 2.0

- London Transport introduced the production Routemaster double-decker bus into public service[119]
- Prestwick and Renfrew Airports became the first in the U.K. with duty-free shops[126]

Alphabetical listing by artist

Artist	Title	Year
Adam Faith	What do you want?	1959
Al Hibbler	Unchained melody	1955
Al Martino	Here in my heart	1952
		1953
Al Martino	Now	1953
Al Martino	Rachel	1953
Al Martino	Take my heart	1952
Al Martino	The man from Laramie	1955
Al Martino	The story of Tina	1954
Al Martino	Wanted	1954
Al Saxon	You're the top cha cha	1959
Alfi & Harry	The trouble with Harry	1956
Alma Cogan	Bell bottom blues	1954
Alma Cogan	Dreamboat	1955
Alma Cogan	Go on by	1955
Alma Cogan	I can't tell a waltz from a tango	1954
		1955
Alma Cogan	In the middle of the house	1956
Alma Cogan	Little things mean a lot	1954
Alma Cogan	Never do a tango with an eskimo	1955
		1956
Alma Cogan	Sugartime	1958
Alma Cogan	The banjo's back in town	1955
Alma Cogan	Twenty tiny fingers	1955
Alma Cogan	Willie can	1956
Alma Cogan	You, me and us	1957
Ames Brothers	The naughty lady of Shady Lane	1955
Andy Williams	Butterfly	1957
Andy Williams	I like your kind of love	1957
Anne Shelton	Arrivederci darling	1955
		1956
Anne Shelton	Lay down your arms	1956
Anne Shelton	Seven days	1956
Anthony Newley	I've waited so long	1959
Anthony Newley	Idle rock-a-boogie	1959
Anthony Newley	Idle on parade	1959

Anthony Newley	Sat'day night rock-a-boogie	1959
Anthony Newley	Personality	1959
Anthony Steel & the Radio Revellers	West of Zanzibar	1954
Art & Dotty Todd	Broken wings	1953
Avons	Seven little girls (sitting in the back seat)	1959
Barbara Lyon	Stowaway	1955
Bernard Bresslaw	Mad passionate love	1958
Bert Weedon	Guitar boogie shuffle	1959
Beverley Sisters	I saw Mommy kissing Santa Claus	1953 1954
Beverley Sisters	Little donkey	1959
Beverley Sisters	Little drummer boy	1959
Beverley Sisters	Freight train	1957
Big Ben Banjo Band	Let's get together again	1955 1956
Big Ben Banjo Band	Let's get together No.1	1954 1955
Big Bopper	Chantilly lace	1959
Bill Haley & His Comets	Don't knock the rock	1957
Bill Haley & His Comets	Mambo rock	1955
Bill Haley & His Comets	Razzle dazzle	1956
Bill Haley & His Comets	Rip it up	1956 1957
Bill Haley & His Comets	Rock around the clock	1955 1956
Bill Haley & His Comets	Rock this joint	1957
Bill Haley & His Comets	Rock-a-beatin' boogie	1956
Bill Haley & His Comets	Rockin' through the rye	1956 1957
Bill Haley & His Comets	See you later alligator	1956
Bill Haley & His Comets	Shake, rattle and roll	1954 1955
Bill Haley & His Comets	The Saints rock 'n' roll	1956
Bill Hayes	The ballad of Davy Crockett	1956
Bill Justis	Raunchy	1958
Billie Anthony	This ole house	1954 1955
Billy Cotton	Puttin' on the style	1957
Billy Cotton Band	Friends and neighbours	1954

Billy Cotton & His Band	I saw Mommy kissing Santa Claus	1953 1954
Billy Cotton & His Band	In a golden coach	1953
Billy Eckstine	Gigi	1959
Billy Eckstine	No one but you	1954 1955
Billy Fury	Maybe tomorrow	1959
Billy May & His Orchestra	Theme from 'The Man With The Golden Arm'	1956
Billy Vaughan Orchestra	The shifting whispering sands	1956
Billy Vaughan Orchestra	Theme from 'The Threepenny Opera'	1956
Billy Ward & The Dominoes	Stardust	1957
Bing Crosby	Around the world	1957
Bing Crosby	Changing partners	1954
Bing Crosby	Count your blessings instead of sheep	1955
Bing Crosby	Silent night	1952 1953
Bing Crosby	Stranger in Paradise	1955
Bing Crosby	The Isle of Innisfree	1952 1953
Bing Crosby & Grace Kelly	True love	1956 1957
Bing Crosby & Jane Wyman	Zing a little zong	1952
Bobby Darin	Dream lover	1959
Bobby Darin	Mack the Knife	1959
Bobby Darin	Splish splash	1958
Bobby Helms	Jacqueline	1958
Bonnie Lou	Tennessee wig walk	1954
Boyd Bennett & His Rockets	Seventeen	1955
Browns	The three bells	1959
Buddy Holly & The Crickets	Early in the morning	1958
Buddy Holly & The Crickets	It doesn't matter anymore	1959
Buddy Holly & The Crickets	Listen to me	1958
Buddy Holly & The Crickets	Maybe baby	1958
Buddy Holly & The Crickets	Oh boy!	1958
Buddy Holly & The Crickets	Peggy Sue	1958
Buddy Holly & The Crickets	Peggy Sue got married	1959
Buddy Holly & The Crickets	Rave on	1958
Buddy Holly & The Crickets	That'll be the day	1957

Buddy Holly & The Crickets	Think it over	1958
Buddy Morrow	Night train	1953
Carl Perkins	Blue suede shoes	1956
Caterina Valente	The breeze and I	1955
Central Band Of The Royal Air Force	Dambusters March	1955
Champs	Tequila	1958
Charlie Applewhite & His Orchestra	Blue Star (Theme from The Medic)	1955
Charlie Drake	Splish splash	1958
Charlie Gracie	Butterfly	1957
Charlie Gracie	Fabulous	1957
Charlie Gracie	I love you so much it hurts	1957
Charlie Gracie	Wanderin' eyes	1957
Charlie Kunz	Piano medley No. 114	1954 1955
Chas McDevitt & Nancy Whiskey	Freight train	1957
Chordettes	Born to be with you	1956
Chordettes	Lollipop	1958
Chordettes	Mr. Sandman	1954 1955
Chris Barber's Jazz Band	Petite Fleur	1959
Chuck Berry	Sweet little sixteen	1958
Cliff Richard & The Drifters	High class baby	1958 1959
Cliff Richard & The Drifters	Living doll	1959
Cliff Richard & The Drifters	Mean streak	1959
Cliff Richard & The Drifters	Move it	1958
Cliff Richard & The Shadows	Dynamite	1959
Cliff Richard & The Shadows	Travellin' light	1959
Coasters	Charlie Brown	1959
Coasters	Poison Ivy	1959
Coasters	Yakety Yak	1958
Connie Francis	Among my souvenirs	1959
Connie Francis	Fallin'	1958
Connie Francis	I'll get by	1958
Connie Francis	I'm sorry I made you cry	1958
Connie Francis	Lipstick on your collar	1959
Connie Francis	My happiness	1959

Connie Francis	Plenty good lovin'	1959
Connie Francis	Stupid cupid	1958
Connie Francis	Carolina moon	1958
Connie Francis	Who's sorry now	1958
Connie Francis	You always hurt the one you love	1959
Conway Twitty	It's only make believe	1958 1959
Conway Twitty	Mona Lisa	1959
Coronets	Twenty tiny fingers	1955
Craig Douglas	A teenager in love	1959
Craig Douglas	Only sixteen	1959
Crew Cuts	Earth angel	1955
Crew Cuts	Sh-boom	1954
Cyril Stapleton	Blue Star (Theme from The Medic)	1955
Cyril Stapleton	Elephant tango	1955
Cyril Stapleton	The Italian Theme	1956
Danny & The Juniors	At the hop	1958
Danny Kaye	Wonderful Copenhagen	1953
Dav King	No other love	1956
Dave King	The story of my life	1958
Dave King & The Keynotes	Memories are made of this	1956
Dave King & The Keynotes	You can't be true to two	1956
David MacBeth	Mr. Blue	1959
David Seville	Witch doctor	1958
David Seville & The Chipmunks	Ragtime Cowboy Joe	1959
David Whitfield	Answer me	1953 1954
David Whitfield	Bridge of sighs	1953
David Whitfield	Ev'rywhere	1955
David Whitfield	Mama	1955
David Whitfield	My September love	1956
David Whitfield	On the street where you live	1958
David Whitfield	Rags to riches	1953 1954
David Whitfield	Santo Natale	1954 1955
David Whitfield	The adoration waltz	1957
David Whitfield	The book	1954

David Whitfield & Mantovani	Beyond the stars	1955
David Whitfield & Mantovani	When you lose the one you love	1955 1956
David Whitfield with Mantovani & His Orchestra	Cara Mia	1954
De Castro Sisters	Teach me tonight	1955
Dean Martin	How do you speak to an angel?	1954
Dean Martin	Kiss	1953
Dean Martin	Let me go lover	1955
Dean Martin	Mambo Italiano	1955
Dean Martin	Memories are made of this	1956
Dean Martin	Return to me	1958
Dean Martin	Sway	1954
Dean Martin	That's amore	1954
Dean Martin	The naughty lady of Shady Lane	1955
Dean Martin	Under the bridges of Paris	1955
Dean Martin	Volare	1958
Dean Martin	Young and foolish	1956
Debbie Reynolds	Tammy	1957
Diamonds	Little darlin'	1957
Diana Decker	Poppa Piccolino	1953 1954
Dick Hyman Trio	Theme from 'The Threepenny Opera'	1956
Dick James	Garden of Eden	1957
Dick James with Stephen James & His Chums	Robin Hood	1956
Dick James with Stephen James & His Chums	The ballad of Davy Crockett	1956
Dickie Valentine	A blossom fell	1955
Dickie Valentine	All the time and everywhere	1953
Dickie Valentine	Broken wings	1953
Dickie Valentine	Christmas alphabet	1955 1956
Dickie Valentine	Christmas island	1956 1957
Dickie Valentine	Endless	1954
Dickie Valentine	I wonder	1955
Dickie Valentine	In a golden coach	1953

Dickie Valentine	Mr. Sandman	1954 1955
Dickie Valentine	One more sunrise	1959
Dickie Valentine	Out of town	1956
Dickie Valentine	The finger of suspicion	1954 1955
Dickie Valentine	The old pianna rag	1955 1956
Dickie Valentine	Venus	1959
Dickie Valentine	Out of town	1956
Domenico Modugno	Volare	1958
Don Charles' Singing Dogs	Oh! Suzanna / medley: Pat-a-cake / Three blind mice / Jingle bells	1955
Don Cherry	Band of gold	1956
Don Cornell	Hold my hand	1954 1955
Don Cornell	Stranger in Paradise	1955
Don Lang	Cloudburst	1955 1956
Don Lang & His Frantic Five	Witch doctor	1958
Don Robertson	The happy whistler	1956
Doris Day	A very precious love	1958
Doris Day	I'll never stop loving you	1955
Doris Day	Love me or leave me	1955
Doris Day	My love and devotion	1952
Doris Day	Ready, willing and able	1955
Doris Day	Secret love	1954
Doris Day	The black hills of Dakota	1954
Doris Day	Whatever will be will be (Que sera sera)	1956
Doris Day & Frankie Laine	Sugarbush	1952 1953
Doris Day & Johnnie Ray	Full time job	1953
Doris Day & Johnnie Ray	Let's walk that-a-way	1953
Doris Day & Johnnie Ray	Ma says, Pa says	1953
Doris Day & the Mellomen	If I give my heart to you	1954
Dorothy Squires	I'm walking behind you	1953
Dreamweavers	It's almost tomorrow	1956
Duane Eddy	Forty miles of bad road	1959
Duane Eddy	Peter Gunn	1959

Duane Eddy	Some kind-a-earthquake	1959
Duane Eddy	Yep!	1959
Duane Eddy	Rebel rouser	1958
Duke Ellington	Skin deep	1954
Eamonn Andrews	The shifting whispering sands	1956
Eartha Kitt	Under the bridges of Paris	1955
Eddie Calvert	Cherry pink and apple blossom white	1955
Eddie Calvert	John and Julie	1955
Eddie Calvert	Mandy (La Panse)	1958
Eddie Calvert	Oh mein papa	1953 1954
Eddie Calvert	Stranger in Paradise	1955
Eddie Calvert	Zambesi	1956
Eddie Cochran	C'mon everybody	1959
Eddie Cochran	Summertime blues	1958
Eddie Fisher	(I'm always hearing) wedding bells	1955
Eddie Fisher	Cindy oh Cindy	1956 1957
Eddie Fisher	Downhearted	1953
Eddie Fisher	Everything I have is yours	1953
Eddie Fisher	I need you now	1954 1955
Eddie Fisher	Oh my papa	1954
Eddie Fisher	Outside of Heaven	1953
Eddie Fisher	Wish you were here	1953 1954
Eddie Fisher & Sally Sweetland	I'm walking behind you	1953
Edmund Hockridge	By the fountains of Rome	1956
Edmund Hockridge	Young and foolish	1956
Edna Savage	Arrivederci darling	1956
Elias & His Zig Zag Jive Flutes	Tom Hark	1958
Ella Fitzgerald	Swingin' shepherd blues	1958
Elmer Bernstein	Staccato's theme	1959
Elvis Presley	(Let me be your) teddy bear	1957
Elvis Presley	A big hunk 'o love	1959
Elvis Presley	A fool such as I	1959
Elvis Presley	I need your love tonight	1959
Elvis Presley	All shook up	1957

Elvis Presley	Blue moon	1956 1957
Elvis Presley	Blue suede shoes	1956
Elvis Presley	Don't	1958
Elvis Presley	Got a lot o' livin' to do	1957
Elvis Presley	Hard headed woman	1958
Elvis Presley	Heartbreak Hotel	1956
Elvis Presley	Hound dog	1956 1957
Elvis Presley	I want you, I need you, I love you	1956
Elvis Presley	Jailhouse rock	1958
Elvis Presley	Young and beautiful	1958
Elvis Presley	I want to be free	1958
Elvis Presley	Don't leave me now	1958
Elvis Presley	(You're so square) Baby I don't care	1958
Elvis Presley	King Creole	1958
Elvis Presley	Lawdy Miss Clawdy	1957
Elvis Presley	Love me tender	1956 1957
Elvis Presley	One night	1959
Elvis Presley	I got stung	1959
Elvis Presley	Paralysed	1957
Elvis Presley	Party	1957 1958
Elvis Presley	Santa bring my baby back to me	1957 1958
Elvis Presley	Too much	1957
Elvis Presley	Trying to get to you	1957
Elvis Presley	Wear my ring around your neck	1958
Emile Ford & The Checkmates	What do you want to make those eyes at me for?	1959
Eve Boswell	Pickin' a chicken	1956
Everly Brothers	(Til) I kissed you	1959
Everly Brothers	All I have to do is dream	1958
Everly Brothers	Claudette	1958
Everly Brothers	Bird dog	1958 1959
Everly Brothers	Bye bye love	1957

Everly Brothers	Poor Jenny	1959
Everly Brothers	Problems	1959
Everly Brothers	Take a message to Mary	1959
Everly Brothers	Wake up little Susie	1957 1958
Fats Domino	Be my guest	1959
Fats Domino	Blueberry Hill	1957
Fats Domino	I want to walk you home	1959
Fats Domino	I'm in love again	1956
Fats Domino	I'm walkin'	1957
Fats Domino	Margie	1959
Fats Domino	The big beat	1958
Ferko String Band	Alabama jubilee	1955
Five Smith Brothers	I'm in favour of friendship	1955
Fleetwoods	Come softly to me	1959
Floyd Robinson	Makin' love	1959
Four Aces	A woman in love	1956
Four Aces	Love is a many splendoured thing	1955 1956
Four Aces	Mr. Sandman	1955
Four Aces	Stranger in Paradise	1955
Four Aces	The world outside	1959
Four Aces	Three coins in the fountain	1954
Four Knights	(Oh baby mine) I get so lonely	1954
Four Preps	Big man	1958
Frank Chacksfield	Ebb tide	1954
Frank Chacksfield	In old Lisbon	1956
Frank Chacksfield	Terry's theme from 'Limelight'	1953
Frank Chacksfield's Tunesmiths	Little red monkey	1953
Frank Sinatra	(Love is) the tender trap	1956
Frank Sinatra	All the way	1957 1958
Frank Sinatra	Chicago	1957 1958
Frank Sinatra	French Foreign Legion	1959
Frank Sinatra	High hopes	1959
Frank Sinatra	Learnin' the blues	1955
Frank Sinatra	Love and marriage	1956
Frank Sinatra	Not as a stranger	1955
Frank Sinatra	Three coins in the fountain	1954

Frank Sinatra	You're getting to be a habit with me	1956
Frank Sinatra	You brought a new kind of love to me	1956
Frank Sinatra	Witchcraft	1958
Frank Sinatra	You my love	1955
Frank Sinatra	Young at heart	1954
Frankie Avalon	Venus	1959
Frankie Laine	A woman in love	1956 1957
Frankie Laine	Answer me	1953 1954
Frankie Laine	Blowing wild	1954
Frankie Laine	Granada	1954
Frankie Laine	Hawkeye	1955 1956
Frankie Laine	Hey Joe	1953
Frankie Laine	High noon (do not forsake me)	1952 1953
Frankie Laine	Hummingbird	1955
Frankie Laine	I believe	1953
Frankie Laine	In the beginning	1955
Frankie Laine	Love is a golden ring	1957
Frankie Laine	Moonlight gambler	1957
Frankie Laine	My friend	1954
Frankie Laine	Rawhide	1959
Frankie Laine	Strange lady in town	1955
Frankie Laine	The girl in the wood	1953
Frankie Laine	The kid's last fight	1954
Frankie Laine	There must be a reason	1954
Frankie Laine	Where the winds blow	1953
Frankie Laine & Jimmy Boyd	Tell me a story	1953
Frankie Laine & The Four Lads	Rain, rain, rain	1954 1955
Frankie Laine & The Mellomen	Cool water	1955
Frankie Laine & The Mellomen	Sixteen tons	1956
Frankie Lymon & The Teenagers	Baby baby	1957
Frankie Lymon & The Teenagers	I'm not a juvenile delinquent	1957
Frankie Lymon & The Teenagers	Why do fools fall in love	1956

Frankie Vaughan	Can't get along without you	1958
Frankie Vaughan	We are not alone	1958
Frankie Vaughan	Garden of Eden	1957
Frankie Vaughan	Green door	1956 1957
Frankie Vaughan	Happy days and lonely nights	1955
Frankie Vaughan	Istanbul (not Constantinople)	1954
Frankie Vaughan	Kewpie doll	1958
Frankie Vaughan	Kisses sweeter than wine	1958
Frankie Vaughan	Man on fire	1957
Frankie Vaughan	Wanderin' eyes	1957
Frankie Vaughan	My boy flat top	1956
Frankie Vaughan	Seventeen	1955
Frankie Vaughan	The heart of a man	1959
Frankie Vaughan	Tweedle dee	1955
Frankie Vaughan & The Kaye Sisters	Come softly to me	1959
Frankie Vaughan & The Kaye Sisters	Gotta have something in the bank Frank	1957
Freddie Bell & The Bellboys	Giddy up a ding dong	1956
Freddy Cannon	Tallahassee Lassie	1959
Gary Miller	Garden of Eden	1957
Gary Miller	Robin Hood	1956
Gary Miller	The story of my life	1958
Gary Miller	The yellow rose of Texas	1955
Gene Vincent	Be-bop-a-lula	1956
Gene Vincent	Blue jean bop	1956
George Melachrino Orchestra	Autumn concerto	1956
Georgia Gibbs	Tweedle dee	1955
Gisele McKenzie	Seven lonely days	1953
Glenn Miller	Moonlight serenade	1954
Gogi Grant	The wayward wind	1956
Goons	I'm walking backwards for Christmas	1956
Goons	Bluebottle blues	1956
Goons	Ying tong song	1956
Goons	Bloodnock's rock & roll call	1956
Gracie Fields	Around the world	1957
Guy Mitchell	A dime and a dollar	1954
Guy Mitchell	Call Rosie on the phone	1957
Guy Mitchell	Knee deep in the blues	1957

Guy Mitchell	Chick-a-boom	1953 1954
Guy Mitchell	Cloud lucky seven	1953 1954
Guy Mitchell	Feet up (pat him on the po-po)	1952 1953
Guy Mitchell	Look at that girl	1953
Guy Mitchell	Pretty little black eyed Susie	1953
Guy Mitchell	Rock-a-billy	1957
Guy Mitchell	She wears red feathers	1953
Guy Mitchell	Singing the blues	1956 1957
Guy Mitchell	Sippin' soda	1954
Guy Mitchell	The cuff of my shirt	1954
Harry Belafonte	Island in the sun	1957
Harry Belafonte	Little Bernadette	1958
Harry Belafonte	Mary's boy child	1957 1958 1959
Harry Belafonte	The banana boat song	1957
Harry Belafonte	The son of Mary	1958
Harry Belafonte & Millard Thomas	Scarlet ribbons	1957
Harry Secombe	On with the motley	1955
Harry Simeone Chorale	Little drummer boy	1959
Hilltoppers	Marianne	1957
Hilltoppers	Only you	1956
Humphrey Lyttleton Band	Bad penny blues	1956
Ink Spots	Melody of love	1955
Jack Scott	My true love	1958
Jackie Dennis	La dee dah	1958
Jackie Wilson	Reet petite	1957 1958
Jane Froman	I wonder	1955
Jane Hutton & Axel Stordahl	Say you're mine again	1953
Jane Morgan	The day the rains came	1958 1959
Jerry Keller	Here comes summer	1959
Jerry Lee Lewis	Breathless	1958
Jerry Lee Lewis	Great balls of fire	1957 1958

Jerry Lee Lewis	High school confidential	1959
Jerry Lee Lewis	Whole lotta shakin' goin' on	1957
Jerry Lewis	Rock-a-bye your baby	1957
Jim Dale	Be my girl	1957 1958
Jim Lowe & The High Fives	Green door	1956
Jimmie Rodgers	Kisses sweeter than wine	1957 1958
Jimmie Rodgers	Oh-oh I'm falling in love again	1958
Jimmie Rodgers	Woman from Liberia	1959
Jimmy Boyd	I saw Mommy kissing Santa Claus	1953 1954
Jimmy Parkinson	In the middle of the house	1956
Jimmy Parkinson	The great pretender	1956
Jimmy Shand Band	Bluebell Polka	1955 1956
Jimmy Young	Chain gang	1956
Jimmy Young	Eternally	1953
Jimmy Young	Faith can move mountains	1953
Jimmy Young	More	1956 1957
Jimmy Young	Someone on your mind	1955 1956
Jimmy Young	The man from Laramie	1955
Jimmy Young	Unchained melody	1955
Jo Stafford	Jambalaya	1952 1953
Jo Stafford	Make love to me	1954
Jo Stafford	Suddenly there's a valley	1955 1956
Jo Stafford	You belong to me	1952 1953
Joan & Rusty Regan	Open up your heart	1955
Joan Regan	If I give my heart to you	1954 1955
Joan Regan	May you always	1959
Joan Regan	Prize of gold	1955
Joan Regan	Ricochet	1953 1954
Joan Regan	Someone else's roses	1954
Joan Regan	My Spetember love	1956

Joan Regan & The Johnston Brothers	Wait for me darling	1954
Joan Weber	Let me go lover	1955
Jodie Sands	Someday (you'll want me to want you)	1958
Joe 'Fingers' Carr	Portuguese washerwoman	1956
Joe 'Mr.Piano' Henderson	Sing it again with Joe	1955
Joe 'Mr.Piano' Henderson	Sing it with Joe	1955
Joe 'Mr.Piano' Henderson	Trudie	1958
Johnnie Ray	Ain't misbehavin'	1956
Johnnie Ray	Build your love	1957
Johnnie Ray	Hernando's hideaway	1955
Johnnie Ray	Hey there	1955
Johnnie Ray	If you believe	1955
Johnnie Ray	Just walkin' in the rain	1956 1957
Johnnie Ray	Look homeward angel	1957
Johnnie Ray	Paths of Paradise	1955
Johnnie Ray	Somebody stole my gal	1953
Johnnie Ray	Song of the dreamer	1955
Johnnie Ray	Such a night	1954
Johnnie Ray	Walkin' my baby back home	1952
Johnnie Ray	Who's sorry now?	1956
Johnnie Ray	Yes tonight, Josephine	1957
Johnnie Ray	You don't owe me a thing	1957
Johnnie Ray	Look homeward angel	1957
Johnnie Ray & The Four Lads	Faith can move mountains	1952 1953
Johnny & The Hurricanes	Red River rock	1959
Johnny Brandon	Don't worry	1955
Johnny Brandon & The Phantoms	Tomorrow	1955
Johnny Dankworth	Experiments with mice	1956
Johnny Duncan	Last train to San Fernando	1957
Johnny Horton	Battle of New Orleans	1959
Johnny Mathis	A certain smile	1958 1959
Johnny Mathis	Someone	1959
Johnny Mathis	Winter wonderland	1959
Johnny Otis Show	Ma, he's making eyes at me	1957 1958

Johnny Otis Show	Bye bye baby	1958
Johnston Brothers	Hernando's hideaway	1955 1956
Johnston Brothers	Oh happy day	1953
Johnston Brothers	Around the world	1957
Johnston Brothers & The George Chisholm Sour-Note Six	Join in and sing again	1956
Joni James	Why don't you believe me?	1953
Judy Garland	The man that got away	1955
Julius La Rosa	Torero	1958
Kalin Twins	When	1958
Kay Starr	Am I a toy or a treasure?	1954
Kay Starr	Changing partners	1954
Kay Starr	Comes-a-long-a-love	1952 1953
Kay Starr	Rock and roll waltz	1956
Kay Starr	Side by side	1953
Ken Mackintosh	Raunchy	1958
Ken Mackintosh	The creep	1954
King Brothers	A white sport coat and a pink carnation	1957
King Brothers	In the middle of an island	1957
Kingston Trio	Tom Dooley	1958 1959
Kitty Kallen	Little things mean a lot	1954
Larry Williams	Bony Moronie	1958
Laurie London	He's got the whole world in his hands	1957 1958
Lee Lawrence	Crying in the chapel	1953 1954
Lee Lawrence	Suddenly there's a valley	1955
Les Baxter & His Orchestra	Unchained melody	1955
Les Paul & Mary Ford	Vaya con dios	1953
Liberace	Unchained melody	1955
Lita Roza	Hey there	1955
Lita Roza	How much is that doggie in the window?	1953
Lita Roza	Jimmy Unknown	1956
Lita Roza	A tear fell	1956
Little Richard	Baby face	1959

Little Richard	By the light of the silvery moon	1959
Little Richard	Good golly Miss Molly	1958
Little Richard	Jenny Jenny	1957
Little Richard	Long tall Sally	1957
Little Richard	Lucille	1957
Little Richard	She's got it	1957
Little Richard	The girl can't help it	1957
Lloyd Price	Personality	1959
Lloyd Price	Stagger Lee	1959
Lloyd Price	Where were you (on our wedding day)?	1959
Lonnie Donegan	Battle of New Orleans	1959
Lonnie Donegan	Bring a little water Sylvie	1956
Lonnie Donegan	Dead or alive	1956
Lonnie Donegan	Cumberland gap	1957
Lonnie Donegan	Does your chewing gum lose its flavour (on the bedpost overnight)	1959
Lonnie Donegan	Don't you rock me Daddy-O	1957
Lonnie Donegan	Fort Worth jail	1959
Lonnie Donegan	Gamblin' man	1957
Lonnie Donegan	Puttin' on the style	1957
Lonnie Donegan	Jack O' Diamonds	1957 1958
Lonnie Donegan	Lost John	1956
Lonnie Donegan	Stewball	1956
Lonnie Donegan	My Dixie darling	1957
Lonnie Donegan	Rock Island line	1956
Lonnie Donegan	Sally don't grieve	1958
Lonnie Donegan	Betty Betty Betty	1958
Lonnie Donegan	Sal's got a sugar lip	1959
Lonnie Donegan	San Miguel	1959
Lonnie Donegan	Railroad Bill	1956
Lonnie Donegan	Stackalee	1956
Lonnie Donegan	The Grand Coolie dam	1958
Lonnie Donegan	Tom Dooley	1958 1959
Lord Rockingham's XI	Hoots mon	1958 1959
Lord Rockingham's XI	Wee Tom	1959

Lou Busch	Zambesi	1956
Louis Armsrong	Takes two to tango	1952 1953
Louis Armstrong	Theme from 'The Threepenny Opera'	1956
Malcolm Vaughan	Chapel of the roses	1957
Malcolm Vaughan	Every day of my life	1955
Malcolm Vaughan	My special angel	1957 1958
Malcolm Vaughan	St.Therese of the Roses	1956 1957
Malcolm Vaughan	Wait for me	1959
Malcolm Vaughan	Willingly	1959
Malcolm Vaughan	With your love	1956
Malcolm Vaughan & The Michael Sammes Singers	More than ever (Come prima)	1958 1959
Malcolm Vaughan & The Michael Sammes Singers	To be loved	1958
Mantovani	Lonely ballerina	1955
Mantovani	White Christmas	1952
Mantovani & His Orchestra	Around the world	1957
Mantovani Orchestra	Swedish Rhapsody	1953 1954
Mantovani Orchestra	Theme from 'Moulin Rouge'	1953
Mantovani Orchestra	White Christmas	1953
Marino Marini Quartet	Come prima	1958 1959
Marino Marini Quartet	Volare	1958
Mario Lanza	Because you're mine	1952 1953
Mario Lanza	I'll walk with God	1955
Mario Lanza	Serenade	1955
Mario Lanza	The drinking song	1955
Marion Ryan	Love me forever	1958
Marty Wilde	A teenager in love	1959
Marty Wilde	Bad boy	1959
Marty Wilde	Donna	1959
Marty Wilde	Endless sleep	1958
Marty Wilde	Sea of love	1959
Marvin Rainwater	I dig you baby	1958
Marvin Rainwater	Whole lotta woman	1958

74

Max Bygraves	(I love to play) my ukelele	1959
Max Bygraves	(The gang that sang) heart of my heart	1954
Max Bygraves	Cowpuncher's cantata	1952 1953
Max Bygraves	Gilly Gilly Ossenfeffer Katzenellen Bogen By The Sea	1954
Max Bygraves	Heart	1957
Max Bygraves	Jingle bell rock	1959
Max Bygraves	Meet me on the corner	1955 1956
Max Bygraves	Mr. Sandman	1955
Max Bygraves	Out of town	1956
Max Bygraves	The ballad of Davy Crockett	1956
Max Bygraves	Tulips from Amsterdam	1958
Max Bygraves	You need hands	1958
Max Bygraves	A white sport coat and a pink carnation	1957
McGuire Sisters	May you always	1959
McGuire Sisters	No more	1955
McGuire Sisters	Sincerely	1955
McGuire Sisters	Sugartime	1958
Mel Torme	Mountain greenery	1956
Michael Flanders	Little drummer boy	1959
Michael Holliday	Hot diggity	1956
Michael Holliday	The gal with the yaller shoes	1956
Michael Holliday	Nothin' to do	1956
Michael Holliday	Stairway of love	1958
Michael Holliday	The gal with the yaller shoes	1956
Michael Holliday	The story of my life	1958
Mike Preston	Mr. Blue	1959
Mills Brothers	Glow worm	1953
Mitch Miller	The yellow rose of Texas	1955 1956
Mitchell Torok	When Mexico gave up the Rhumba	1956 1957
Morris Stoloff	Theme from 'Picnic'	1956
Mudlarks	Book of love	1958
Mudlarks	Lollipop	1958
Muriel Smith	Hold me, thrill me, kiss me	1953
Nat 'King' Cole	A blossom fell	1955

Nat 'King' Cole	Because you're mine	1952 1953
Nat 'King' Cole	Can't I?	1953
Nat 'King' Cole	Dreams can tell a lie	1956
Nat 'King' Cole	Faith can move mountains	1953
Nat 'King' Cole	Love me as though there were no tomorrow	1956
Nat 'King' Cole	Make her mine	1954
Nat 'King' Cole	Mother Nature and Father Time	1953
Nat 'King' Cole	My one sin	1955
Nat 'King' Cole	Pretend	1953
Nat 'King' Cole	Smile	1954
Nat 'King' Cole	Somewhere along the way	1952 1953
Nat 'King' Cole	Tenderly	1954
Nat 'King' Cole	Too young to go steady	1956
Nat 'King' Cole	When I fall in love	1957
Neil Sedaka	I go ape	1959
Neil Sedaka	Oh Carol	1959
Norman Brooks	A sky blue shirt and a rainbow tie	1954
Norman Wisdom	Don't laugh at me ('cause I'm a fool)	1954
Norman Wisdom	The wisdom of a fool	1957
Obernkirchen Children's Choir	The happy wanderer	1954
Olympics	Western movies	1958
Original Cast Of The Army Game	Theme from 'The Army Game'	1958
Pat Boone	A wonderful time up there	1958
Pat Boone	Ain't that a shame	1955 1956
Pat Boone	April love	1957 1958
Pat Boone	Don't forbid me	1957
Pat Boone	For a penny	1959
Pat Boone	Friendly persuasion	1956 1957
Pat Boone	I almost lost my mind	1956
Pat Boone	If dreams came true	1958
Pat Boone	I'll remember tonight	1959

Pat Boone	I'll be home	1956 1957
Pat Boone	It's too soon to know	1958
Pat Boone	Long tall Sally	1956
Pat Boone	Love letters in the sand	1957
Pat Boone	Remember you're mine	1957 1958
Pat Boone	There's a gold mine in the sky	1957 1958
Pat Boone	Sugar moon	1958
Pat Boone	Twixt twelve and twenty	1959
Pat Boone	Why baby why	1957
Patti Page	How much is that doggie in the window?	1953
Paul Anka	(All of a sudden) my heart sings	1959
Paul Anka	Diana	1957 1958
Paul Anka	I love you baby	1957 1958
Paul Anka	Lonely boy	1959
Paul Anka	Put your head on my shoulder	1959
Paul Anka	You are my destiny	1958
Pearl Carr & Teddy Johnson	Sing little birdie	1959
Peggy Lee	Fever	1958
Peggy Lee	Mr. Wonderful	1957
Perez Prado	Cherry pink and apple blossom white	1955
Perez Prado	Patricia	1958
Perry Como	Catch a falling star	1958
Perry Como	Don't let the stars get in your eyes	1953
Perry Como	Glendora	1956
Perry Como	Hot diggity	1956
Perry Como	I know	1959
Perry Como	I may never pass this way again	1958
Perry Como	Idle gossip	1954
Perry Como	Kewpie doll	1958
Perry Como	Love makes the world go round	1958 1959

Perry Como	Magic moments	1958
Perry Como	Mandolins in the moonlight	1958
		1959
Perry Como	Moon talk	1958
Perry Como	More	1956
Perry Como	Papa loves mambo	1954
Perry Como	Tomboy	1959
Perry Como	Wanted	1954
Peter Sellers	Any old iron	1957
Petula Clark	Alone	1957
		1958
Petula Clark	Baby lover	1958
Petula Clark	Majorca	1955
Petula Clark	Suddenly there's a valley	1955
		1956
Petula Clark	The little shoemaker	1954
Petula Clark	With all my heart	1957
Platters	I'm sorry	1957
Platters	My prayer	1956
		1957
Platters	Smoke gets in your eyes	1959
Platters	The great pretender	1956
		1957
Platters	Only you	1956
		1957
Platters	Twilight time	1958
Poni-Tails	Born too late	1958
Ray Anthony & His Orchestra	Dragnet	1953
		1954
Ray Burns	Mobile	1955
Ray Burns & The Coronets	That's how a love song was born	1955
Ray Martin	Blue Tango	1952
Ray Martin Concert Orchestra	Swedish Rhapsody	1953
		1954
Reg Owen	Manhattan spiritual	1959
Ricky Nelson	It's late	1959
Ricky Nelson	Just a little too much	1959
Ricky Nelson	Never be anyone else but you	1959
Ricky Nelson	Poor little fool	1958
Ricky Nelson	Sweeter than you	1959

Ricky Nelson	Someday	1958 1959
Robert Earl	I may never pass this way again	1958
Robert Earl	The wonderful secret of love	1959
Ron Goodwin	Terry's theme from 'Limelight'	1953
Ron Goodwin & His Orchestra	Blue Star (Theme from The Medic)	1955
Ronnie Carroll	The wisdom of a fool	1957
Ronnie Carroll	Walk hand in hand	1956
Ronnie Harris	The story of Tina	1954
Ronnie Hilton	A blossom fell	1955
Ronnie Hilton	Around the world	1957
Ronnie Hilton	I still believe	1954 1955
Ronnie Hilton	No other love	1956
Ronnie Hilton	Stars shine in your eyes	1955
Ronnie Hilton	The yellow rose of Texas	1955
Ronnie Hilton	Two different worlds	1956 1957
Ronnie Hilton	Veni, vidi, vici	1954 1955
Ronnie Hilton	Who are we	1956
Ronnie Hilton	Young and foolish	1956
Ronnie Hilton & The Mike Sammes Singers	The world outside	1959
Rosemary Clooney	Half as much	1952 1953
Rosemary Clooney	Hey there	1955
Rosemary Clooney	Mangos	1957
Rosemary Clooney	This ole house	1954 1955
Rosemary Clooney & Jose Ferrer	Man / Woman (uh-huh)	1954
Rosemary Clooney & The Mellomen	Mambo Italiano	1954 1955
Rosemary Clooney & The Mellomen	Where will the dimple be?	1955
Rosemary June	I'll be with you in apple blossom time	1959
Ruby Murray	Evermore	1955

Ruby Murray	Goodbye Jimmy, goodbye	1959
Ruby Murray	Happy days and lonely nights	1955
Ruby Murray	Heartbeat	1954 1955
Ruby Murray	I'll come when you call	1955
Ruby Murray	Let me go lover	1955
Ruby Murray	Real love	1958 1959
Ruby Murray	Softly, softly	1955
Ruby Murray	You are my first love	1956
Ruby Murray & Anne Warren	If anyone finds this, I love you	1955
Ruby Wright	Bimbo	1954
Ruby Wright	Three stars	1959
Russ Conway	China tea	1959
Russ Conway	More and more party pops	1959
Russ Conway	More party pops	1958 1959
Russ Conway	Roulette	1959
Russ Conway	Side saddle	1959
Russ Conway	Snow coach	1959
Russ Hamilton	We will make love	1957
Russ Hamilton	Wedding ring	1957
Sal Mineo	Start movin' (in my direction)	1957
Sammy Davis Jr.	Hey there	1955
Sammy Davis Jr.	Love me or leave me	1955
Sammy Davis Jr.	Something's gotta give	1955
Sammy Davis Jr.	That old black magic	1955
Sandy Nelson	Teen beat	1959
Sarah Vaughan	Broken-hearted melody	1959
Sheb Wooley	Purple people eater	1958
Shepherd Sisters	Alone	1957
Shirley Bassey	As I love you	1959
Shirley Bassey	Kiss me, honey honey, kiss me	1959
Shirley Bassey	The banana boat song	1957
Slim Dusty	A pub with no beer	1959
Slim Whitman	China doll	1955
Slim Whitman	I'll take you home again, Kathleen	1957
Slim Whitman	I'm a fool	1956
Slim Whitman	Indian love call	1955

Slim Whitman	Rose Marie	1955
Slim Whitman	Serenade	1956
Slim Whitman	Tumbling tumbleweeds	1956
Sonny James	Young love	1957
Southlanders	Alone	1957 1958
Stan Freberg	Sh-boom	1954
Stargazers	Broken wings	1953
Stargazers	Close the door	1955
Stargazers	I see the moon	1954
Stargazers	Somebody	1955
Stargazers	The Crazy Otto rag	1955
Stargazers	The happy wanderer	1954
Stargazers	Twenty tiny fingers	1955 1956
Suzi Miller & The Johnston Brothers	Happy days and lonely nights	1955
Tab Hunter	99 ways	1957
Tab Hunter	Young love	1957
Tarriers	The banana boat song	1957
Ted Heath & His Music	Dragnet	1953 1954
Ted Heath & His Music	Hot toddy	1953
Ted Heath & His Music	Skin deep	1954
Ted Heath & His Music	Swingin' shepherd blues	1958
Ted Heath & His Music	The faithful Hussar	1956
Ted Heath & His Music	Vanessa	1953
Teddy Bears	To know him is to love him	1959
Tennessee Ernie Ford	Give me your word	1955
Tennessee Ernie Ford	Sixteen tons	1956
Tennessee Ernie Ford	The ballad of Davy Crockett	1956
Teresa Brewer	A sweet old-fashioned girl	1956
Teresa Brewer	A tear fell	1956
Teresa Brewer & The Lancers	Let me go lover	1955
Terry Dene	A white sport coat and a pink carnation	1957
Terry Dene	Stairway of love	1958
Tex Ritter	The wayward wind	1956
Three Kayes	Ivory tower	1956
Tommy Dorsey Orchestra feat. Warren Covington	Tea for two cha-cha	1958 1959

Tommy Edwards	It's all in the game	1958
		1959
Tommy Steele	Butterfingers	1957
Tommy Steele	Come on let's go	1958
		1959
Tommy Steele	Happy guitar	1958
Tommy Steele	Knee deep in the blues	1957
Tommy Steele	Little white bull	1959
Tommy Steele	Nairobi	1958
Tommy Steele	Rock with the caveman	1956
Tommy Steele	Shiralee	1957
Tommy Steele	Singing the blues	1956
		1957
Tommy Steele	Tallahassee Lassie	1959
Tommy Steele	The only man on the island	1958
Tommy Steele	Water water	1957
Tommy Steele	A handful of songs	1957
Tommy Steele	Butterfly	1957
Tony Bennett	Close your eyes	1955
Tony Bennett	Stranger in Paradise	1955
Tony Brent	Cindy oh Cindy	1956
		1957
Tony Brent	Dark moon	1957
Tony Brent	Girl of my dreams	1958
Tony Brent	Got you on my mind	1953
Tony Brent	Make it soon	1953
Tony Brent	The clouds will soon roll by	1958
Tony Brent	Walkin' to Missouri	1952
		1953
Tony Martin	Stranger in Paradise	1955
Tony Martin	Walk hand in hand	1956
Vera Lynn	A house with love in it	1956
		1957
Vera Lynn	Auf wiederseh'n sweetheart	1952
Vera Lynn	Forget me not	1952
		1953
Vera Lynn	My son, my son	1954
		1955
Vera Lynn	The homing waltz	1952
Vera Lynn	The Windsor waltz	1953
Vera Lynn	Travellin' home	1957

Vic Damone	On the street where you live	1958
Vipers Skiffle Group	Cumberland gap	1957
Vipers Skiffle Group	Don't you rock me Daddy-O	1957
Vivian Blaine	A bushel and a peck	1953
Winifred Atwell	Theme from "A Threepenny Opera"	1956
Winifred Atwell	Britannia Rag	1952 1953
Winifred Atwell	Coronation rag	1953
Winifred Atwell	Flirtation waltz	1953
Winifred Atwell	Left bank	1956
Winifred Atwell	Let's have a ball	1957 1958
Winifred Atwell	Let's have a ding dong	1955 1956
Winifred Atwell	Let's have a party	1953 1954 1955
Winifred Atwell	Let's have another party	1954 1955
Winifred Atwell	Make it a party	1956 1957
Winifred Atwell	Piano party	1959
Winifred Atwell	Poor people of Paris	1956
Winifred Atwell	The story of three loves (Rachmaninoff's 18th variation on a theme by Paganini)	1954
Winifred Atwell & Frank Chaksfield	Port-Au-Prince	1956
Wink Martindale	Deck of cards	1959

Alphabetical listing by title

Title	Artist	Year
(All of a sudden) my heart sings	Paul Anka	1959
(I love to play) my ukelele	Max Bygraves	1959
(I'm always hearing) wedding bells	Eddie Fisher	1955
(Let me be your) teddy bear	Elvis Presley	1957
(Love is) the tender trap	Frank Sinatra	1956
(Oh baby mine) I get so lonely	Four Knights	1954
(The gang that sang) heart of my heart	Max Bygraves	1954
(Til) I kissed you	Everly Brothers	1959
(You're so square) Baby I don't care	Elvis Presley	1958
99 ways	Tab Hunter	1957
A big hunk 'o love	Elvis Presley	1959
A blossom fell	Dickie Valentine	1955
A blossom fell	Nat 'King' Cole	1955
A blossom fell	Ronnie Hilton	1955
A bushel and a peck	Vivian Blaine	1953
A certain smile	Johnny Mathis	1958 1959
A dime and a dollar	Guy Mitchell	1954
A fool such as I	Elvis Presley	1959
A handful of songs	Tommy Steele	1957
A house with love in it	Vera Lynn	1956 1957
A pub with no beer	Slim Dusty	1959
A sky blue shirt and a rainbow tie	Norman Brooks	1954
A sweet old-fashioned girl	Teresa Brewer	1956
A tear fell	Lita Roza	1956
A tear fell	Teresa Brewer	1956
A teenager in love	Craig Douglas	1959
A teenager in love	Marty Wilde	1959
A very precious love	Doris Day	1958
A white sport coat and a pink carnation	King Brothers	1957

A white sport coat and a pink carnation	Max Bygraves	1957
A white sport coat and a pink carnation	Terry Dene	1957
A woman in love	Four Aces	1956
A woman in love	Frankie Laine	1956 1957
A wonderful time up there	Pat Boone	1958
Ain't misbehavin'	Johnnie Ray	1956
Ain't that a shame	Pat Boone	1955 1956
Alabama jubilee	Ferko String Band	1955
All I have to do is dream	Everly Brothers	1958
All shook up	Elvis Presley	1957
All the time and everywhere	Dickie Valentine	1953
All the way	Frank Sinatra	1957 1958
All the way	Frank Sinatra	1958
Alone	Petula Clark	1957 1958
Alone	Shepherd Sisters	1957
Alone	Southlanders	1957 1958
Am I a toy or a treasure?	Kay Starr	1954
Among my souvenirs	Connie Francis	1959
Answer me	David Whitfield	1953 1954
Answer me	Frankie Laine	1953 1954
Any old iron	Peter Sellers	1957
April love	Pat Boone	1957 1958
Around the world	Bing Crosby	1957
Around the world	Gracie Fields	1957
Around the world	Johnston Brothers	1957
Around the world	Mantovani & His Orchestra	1957
Around the world	Ronnie Hilton	1957
Arrivederci darling	Anne Shelton	1955 1956
Arrivederci darling	Edna Savage	1956
As I love you	Shirley Bassey	1959

At the hop	Danny & The Juniors	1958
Auf wiederseh'n sweetheart	Vera Lynn	1952
Autumn concerto	George Melachrino Orchestra	1956
Baby baby	Frankie Lymon & The Teenagers	1957
Baby face	Little Richard	1959
Baby lover	Petula Clark	1958
Bad boy	Marty Wilde	1959
Bad penny blues	Humphrey Lyttleton Band	1956
Band of gold	Don Cherry	1956
Battle of New Orleans	Johnny Horton	1959
Battle of New Orleans	Lonnie Donegan	1959
Be my girl	Jim Dale	1957 1958
Be my guest	Fats Domino	1959
Be-bop-a-lula	Gene Vincent	1956
Because you're mine	Mario Lanza	1952 1953
Because you're mine	Nat 'King' Cole	1952 1953
Bell bottom blues	Alma Cogan	1954
Betty Betty Betty	Lonnie Donegan	1958
Beyond the stars	David Whitfield & Mantovani	1955
Big man	Four Preps	1958
Bimbo	Ruby Wright	1954
Bird dog	Everly Brothers	1958 1959
Bloodnock's rock & roll call	Goons	1956
Blowing wild	Frankie Laine	1954
Bluebottle blues	Goons	1956
Blue jean bop	Gene Vincent	1956
Blue moon	Elvis Presley	1956 1957
Blue Star (Theme from The Medic)	Charlie Applewhite & His Orchestra	1955
Blue Star (Theme from The Medic)	Cyril Stapleton	1955
Blue Star (Theme from The Medic)	Ron Goodwin & His Orchestra	1955

Blue suede shoes	Carl Perkins	1956
Blue suede shoes	Elvis Presley	1956
Blue Tango	Ray Martin	1952
Bluebell Polka	Jimmy Shand Band	1955 1956
Blueberry Hill	Fats Domino	1957
Bony Moronie	Larry Williams	1958
Book of love	Mudlarks	1958
Born to be with you	Chordettes	1956
Born too late	Poni-Tails	1958
Breathless	Jerry Lee Lewis	1958
Bridge of sighs	David Whitfield	1953
Bring a little water Sylvie	Lonnie Donegan	1956
Britannia Rag	Winifred Atwell	1952 1953
Broken wings	Art & Dotty Todd	1953
Broken wings	Dickie Valentine	1953
Broken wings	Stargazers	1953
Broken-hearted melody	Sarah Vaughan	1959
Build your love	Johnnie Ray	1957
Butterfingers	Tommy Steele	1957
Butterfly	Andy Williams	1957
Butterfly	Charlie Gracie	1957
Butterfly	Tommy Steele	1957
By the fountains of Rome	Edmund Hockridge	1956
By the light of the silvery moon	Little Richard	1959
Bye bye baby	Johnny Otis Show	1958
Bye bye love	Everly Brothers	1957
Call Rosie on the phone	Guy Mitchell	1957
Can't get along without you	Frankie Vaughan	1958
Can't I?	Nat 'King' Cole	1953
Cara Mia	David Whitfield with Mantovani & His Orchestra	1954
Carolina moon	Connie Francis	1958
Catch a falling star	Perry Como	1958
Chain gang	Jimmy Young	1956
Changing partners	Bing Crosby	1954
Changing partners	Kay Starr	1954
Chantilly lace	Big Bopper	1959
Chapel of the roses	Malcolm Vaughan	1957
Charlie Brown	Coasters	1959

Cherry pink and apple blossom white	Eddie Calvert	1955
Cherry pink and apple blossom white	Perez Prado	1955
Chicago	Frank Sinatra	1957 1958
Chick-a-boom	Guy Mitchell	1953 1954
China doll	Slim Whitman	1955
China tea	Russ Conway	1959
Christmas alphabet	Dickie Valentine	1955 1956
Christmas island	Dickie Valentine	1956 1957
Cindy oh Cindy	Eddie Fisher	1956 1957
Cindy oh Cindy	Tony Brent	1956 1957
Claudette	Everly Brothers	1958
Close the door	Stargazers	1955
Close your eyes	Tony Bennett	1955
Cloud lucky seven	Guy Mitchell	1953 1954
Cloudburst	Don Lang	1955 1956
C'mon everybody	Eddie Cochran	1959
Come on let's go	Tommy Steele	1958 1959
Come prima	Marino Marini Quartet	1958 1959
Come softly to me	Fleetwoods	1959
Come softly to me	Frankie Vaughan & The Kaye Sisters	1959
Comes a-long-a-love	Kay Starr	1952 1953
Cool water	Frankie Laine & The Mellomen	1955
Coronation rag	Winifred Atwell	1953
Count your blessings instead of sheep	Bing Crosby	1955
Cowpuncher's cantata	Max Bygraves	1952 1953

Crying in the chapel	Lee Lawrence	1953 1954
Cumberland gap	Lonnie Donegan	1957
Cumberland gap	Vipers Skiffle Group	1957
Dambusters March	Central Band Of The Royal Air Force	1955
Dark moon	Tony Brent	1957
Dead or alive	Lonnie Donegan	1956
Deck of cards	Wink Martindale	1959
Diana	Paul Anka	1957 1958
Does your chewing gum lose its flavour (on the bedpost overnight)	Lonnie Donegan	1959
Donna	Marty Wilde	1959
Don't	Elvis Presley	1958
Don't forbid me	Pat Boone	1957
Don't knock the rock	Bill Haley & His Comets	1957
Don't laugh at me ('cause I'm a fool)	Norman Wisdom	1954
Don't leave me now	Elvis Presley	1958
Don't let the stars get in your eyes	Perry Como	1953
Don't worry	Johnny Brandon	1955
Don't you rock me Daddy-O	Lonnie Donegan	1957
Don't you rock me Daddy-O	Vipers Skiffle Group	1957
Downhearted	Eddie Fisher	1953
Dragnet	Ray Anthony & His Orchestra	1953 1954
Dragnet	Ted Heath & His Music	1953 1954
Dream lover	Bobby Darin	1959
Dreamboat	Alma Cogan	1955
Dreams can tell a lie	Nat 'King' Cole	1956
Dynamite	Cliff Richard & The Shadows	1959
Early in the morning	Buddy Holly & The Crickets	1958
Earth angel	Crew Cuts	1955
Ebb tide	Frank Chacksfield	1954
Elephant tango	Cyril Stapleton	1955
Endless	Dickie Valentine	1954
Endless sleep	Marty Wilde	1958
Eternally	Jimmy Young	1953

Evermore	Ruby Murray	1955
Every day of my life	Malcolm Vaughan	1955
Everything I have is yours	Eddie Fisher	1953
Ev'rywhere	David Whitfield	1955
Experiments with mice	Johnny Dankworth	1956
Fabulous	Charlie Gracie	1957
Faith can move mountains	Jimmy Young	1953
Faith can move mountains	Johnnie Ray & The Four Lads	1952 1953
Faith can move mountains	Nat 'King' Cole	1953
Fallin'	Connie Francis	1958
Feet up (pat him on the po-po)	Guy Mitchell	1952 1953
Fever	Peggy Lee	1958
Flirtation waltz	Winifred Atwell	1953
For a penny	Pat Boone	1959
Forget me not	Vera Lynn	1952 1953
Fort Worth jail	Lonnie Donegan	1959
Forty miles of bad road	Duane Eddy	1959
Freight train	Beverley Sisters	1957
Freight train	Chas McDevitt & Nancy Whiskey	1957
French Foreign Legion	Frank Sinatra	1959
Friendly persuasion	Pat Boone	1956 1957
Friends and neighbours	Billy Cotton Band	1954
Full time job	Doris Day & Johnnie Ray	1953
Gamblin' man	Lonnie Donegan	1957
Garden of Eden	Dick James	1957
Garden of Eden	Frankie Vaughan	1957
Garden of Eden	Gary Miller	1957
Giddy up a ding dong	Freddie Bell & The Bellboys	1956
Gigi	Billy Eckstine	1959
Gilly Gilly Ossenfeffer Katzenellen Bogen By The Sea	Max Bygraves	1954
Girl of my dreams	Tony Brent	1958
Give me your word	Tennessee Ernie Ford	1955
Glendora	Perry Como	1956

Glow worm	Mills Brothers	1953
Go on by	Alma Cogan	1955
Good golly Miss Molly	Little Richard	1958
Goodbye Jimmy, goodbye	Ruby Murray	1959
Got a lot o' livin' to do	Elvis Presley	1957
Got you on my mind	Tony Brent	1953
Gotta have something in the bank Frank	Frankie Vaughan & The Kaye Sisters	1957
Granada	Frankie Laine	1954
Great balls of fire	Jerry Lee Lewis	1957 1958
Green door	Frankie Vaughan	1956 1957
Green door	Jim Lowe & The High Fives	1956
Guitar boogie shuffle	Bert Weedon	1959
Half as much	Rosemary Clooney	1952 1953
Happy days and lonely nights	Frankie Vaughan	1955
Happy days and lonely nights	Ruby Murray	1955
Happy days and lonely nights	Suzi Miller & The Johnston Brothers	1955
Happy guitar	Tommy Steele	1958
Hard headed woman	Elvis Presley	1958
Hawkeye	Frankie Laine	1955 1956
Heart	Max Bygraves	1957
Heartbeat	Ruby Murray	1954 1955
Heartbreak Hotel	Elvis Presley	1956
Here comes summer	Jerry Keller	1959
Here in my heart	Al Martino	1952 1953
Hernando's hideaway	Johnnie Ray	1955
Hernando's hideaway	Johnston Brothers	1955 1956
He's got the whole world in his hands	Laurie London	1957 1958
Hey Joe	Frankie Laine	1953
Hey there	Johnnie Ray	1955
Hey there	Lita Roza	1955
Hey there	Rosemary Clooney	1955

Hey there	Sammy Davis Jr.	1955
High class baby	Cliff Richard & The Drifters	1958
		1959
High hopes	Frank Sinatra	1959
High noon (do not forsake me)	Frankie Laine	1952
		1953
High school confidential	Jerry Lee Lewis	1959
Hold me, thrill me, kiss me	Muriel Smith	1953
Hold my hand	Don Cornell	1954
		1955
Hoots mon	Lord Rockingham's XI	1958
		1959
Hot diggity	Perry Como	1956
Hot diggity	Michael Holliday	1956
Hot toddy	Ted Heath & His Music	1953
Hound dog	Elvis Presley	1956
		1957
How do you speak to an angel?	Dean Martin	1954
How much is that doggie in the window?	Lita Roza	1953
How much is that doggie in the window?	Patti Page	1953
Hummingbird	Frankie Laine	1955
I almost lost my mind	Pat Boone	1956
I believe	Frankie Laine	1953
I can't tell a waltz from a tango	Alma Cogan	1954
		1955
I dig you baby	Marvin Rainwater	1958
I go ape	Neil Sedaka	1959
I got stung	Elvis Presley	1959
I know	Perry Como	1959
I like your kind of love	Andy Williams	1957
I love you baby	Paul Anka	1957
		1958
I love you so much it hurts	Charlie Gracie	1957
I may never pass this way again	Perry Como	1958
I may never pass this way again	Robert Earl	1958
I need you now	Eddie Fisher	1954
		1955
I need your love tonight	Elvis Presley	1959

I saw Mommy kissing Santa Claus	Beverley Sisters	1953 1954
I saw Mommy kissing Santa Claus	Billy Cotton & His Band	1953 1954
I saw Mommy kissing Santa Claus	Jimmy Boyd	1953 1954
I see the moon	Stargazers	1954
I still believe	Ronnie Hilton	1954 1955
I want to be free	Elvis Presley	1958
I want to walk you home	Fats Domino	1959
I want you, I need you, I love you	Elvis Presley	1956
I wonder	Dickie Valentine	1955
I wonder	Jane Froman	1955
Idle gossip	Perry Como	1954
Idle on parade	Anthony Newley	1959
Idle rock-a-boogie	Anthony Newley	1959
If anyone finds this, I love you	Ruby Murray & Anne Warren	1955
If dreams came true	Pat Boone	1958
If I give my heart to you	Doris Day & the Mellomen	1954
If I give my heart to you	Joan Regan	1954 1955
If you believe	Johnnie Ray	1955
I'll be home	Pat Boone	1956 1957
I'll be with you in apple blossom time	Rosemary June	1959
I'll come when you call	Ruby Murray	1955
I'll get by	Connie Francis	1958
I'll never stop loving you	Doris Day	1955
I'll remember tonight	Pat Boone	1959
I'll take you home again, Kathleen	Slim Whitman	1957
I'll walk with God	Mario Lanza	1955
I'm a fool	Slim Whitman	1956
I'm in favour of friendship	Five Smith Brothers	1955
I'm in love again	Fats Domino	1956
I'm not a juvenile delinquent	Frankie Lymon & The Teenagers	1957
I'm sorry	Platters	1957

I'm sorry I made you cry	Connie Francis	1958
I'm walkin'	Fats Domino	1957
I'm walking backwards for Christmas	Goons	1956
I'm walking behind you	Dorothy Squires	1953
I'm walking behind you	Eddie Fisher & Sally Sweetland	1953
In a golden coach	Billy Cotton & His Band	1953
In a golden coach	Dickie Valentine	1953
In old Lisbon	Frank Chacksfield	1956
In the beginning	Frankie Laine	1955
In the middle of an island	King Brothers	1957
In the middle of the house	Alma Cogan	1956
In the middle of the house	Jimmy Parkinson	1956
Indian love call	Slim Whitman	1955
Island in the sun	Harry Belafonte	1957
Istanbul (not Constantinople)	Frankie Vaughan	1954
It doesn't matter anymore	Buddy Holly & The Crickets	1959
It's all in the game	Tommy Edwards	1958 1959
It's almost tomorrow	Dreamweavers	1956
It's late	Ricky Nelson	1959
It's only make believe	Conway Twitty	1958 1959
It's too soon to know	Pat Boone	1958
I've waited so long	Anthony Newley	1959
Ivory tower	Three Kayes	1956
Jack O' Diamonds	Lonnie Donegan	1957 1958
Jacqueline	Bobby Helms	1958
Jailhouse rock	Elvis Presley	1958
Jambalaya	Jo Stafford	1952 1953
Jenny Jenny	Little Richard	1957
Jimmy Unknown	Lita Roza	1956
Jingle bell rock	Max Bygraves	1959
John and Julie	Eddie Calvert	1955
Join in and sing again	Johnston Brothers & The George Chisholm Sour-Note Six	1956
Just a little too much	Ricky Nelson	1959

Just walkin' in the rain	Johnnie Ray	1956 1957
Kewpie doll	Frankie Vaughan	1958
Kewpie doll	Perry Como	1958
King Creole	Elvis Presley	1958
Kiss	Dean Martin	1953
Kiss me, honey honey, kiss me	Shirley Bassey	1959
Kisses sweeter than wine	Frankie Vaughan	1958
Kisses sweeter than wine	Jimmie Rodgers	1957 1958
Knee deep in the blues	Guy Mitchell	1957
Knee deep in the blues	Tommy Steele	1957
La dee dah	Jackie Dennis	1958
Last train to San Fernando	Johnny Duncan	1957
Lawdy Miss Clawdy	Elvis Presley	1957
Lay down your arms	Anne Shelton	1956
Learnin' the blues	Frank Sinatra	1955
Left bank	Winifred Atwell	1956
Let me go lover	Dean Martin	1955
Let me go lover	Joan Weber	1955
Let me go lover	Ruby Murray	1955
Let me go lover	Teresa Brewer & The Lancers	1955
Let's get together again	Big Ben Banjo Band	1955 1956
Let's get together No.1	Big Ben Banjo Band	1954 1955
Let's have a ball	Winifred Atwell	1957 1958
Let's have a ding dong	Winifred Atwell	1955 1956
Let's have a party	Winifred Atwell	1953 1954 1955
Let's have another party	Winifred Atwell	1954 1955
Let's walk that-a-way	Doris Day & Johnnie Ray	1953
Lipstick on your collar	Connie Francis	1959
Listen to me	Buddy Holly & The Crickets	1958
Little Bernadette	Harry Belafonte	1958
Little darlin'	Diamonds	1957
Little donkey	Beverley Sisters	1959

Little drummer boy	Beverley Sisters	1959
Little drummer boy	Harry Simeone Chorale	1959
Little drummer boy	Michael Flanders	1959
Little red monkey	Frank Chacksfield's Tunesmiths	1953
Little things mean a lot	Alma Cogan	1954
Little things mean a lot	Kitty Kallen	1954
Little white bull	Tommy Steele	1959
Living doll	Cliff Richard & The Drifters	1959
Lollipop	Chordettes	1958
Lollipop	Mudlarks	1958
Lonely ballerina	Mantovani	1955
Lonely boy	Paul Anka	1959
Long tall Sally	Little Richard	1957
Long tall Sally	Pat Boone	1956
Look at that girl	Guy Mitchell	1953
Look homeward angel	Johnnie Ray	1957
Look homeward angel	Johnnie Ray	1957
Lost John	Lonnie Donegan	1956
Love and marriage	Frank Sinatra	1956
Love is a golden ring	Frankie Laine	1957
Love is a many splendoured thing	Four Aces	1955 1956
Love letters in the sand	Pat Boone	1957
Love makes the world go round	Perry Como	1958 1959
Love me as though there were no tomorrow	Nat 'King' Cole	1956
Love me forever	Marion Ryan	1958
Love me or leave me	Doris Day	1955
Love me or leave me	Sammy Davis Jr.	1955
Love me tender	Elvis Presley	1956 1957
Lucille	Little Richard	1957
Ma says, Pa says	Doris Day & Johnnie Ray	1953
Ma, he's making eyes at me	Johnny Otis Show	1957 1958
Mack the Knife	Bobby Darin	1959
Mad passionate love	Bernard Bresslaw	1958
Magic moments	Perry Como	1958
Majorca	Petula Clark	1955

Make her mine	Nat 'King' Cole	1954
Make it a party	Winifred Atwell	1956
		1957
Make it soon	Tony Brent	1953
Make love to me	Jo Stafford	1954
Makin' love	Floyd Robinson	1959
Mama	David Whitfield	1955
Mambo Italiano	Dean Martin	1955
Mambo Italiano	Rosemary Clooney & The Mellomen	1954
		1955
Mambo rock	Bill Haley & His Comets	1955
Man / Woman (uh-huh)	Rosemary Clooney & Jose Ferrer	1954
Man on fire	Frankie Vaughan	1957
Mandolins in the moonlight	Perry Como	1958
		1959
Mandy (La Panse)	Eddie Calvert	1958
Mangos	Rosemary Clooney	1957
Manhattan spiritual	Reg Owen	1959
Margie	Fats Domino	1959
Marianne	Hilltoppers	1957
Mary's boy child	Harry Belafonte	1957
		1958
		1959
May you always	Joan Regan	1959
May you always	McGuire Sisters	1959
Maybe baby	Buddy Holly & The Crickets	1958
Maybe tomorrow	Billy Fury	1959
Mean streak	Cliff Richard & The Drifters	1959
Meet me on the corner	Max Bygraves	1955
		1956
Melody of love	Ink Spots	1955
Memories are made of this	Dave King & The Keynotes	1956
Memories are made of this	Dean Martin	1956
Mobile	Ray Burns	1955
Mona Lisa	Conway Twitty	1959
Moon talk	Perry Como	1958
Moonlight gambler	Frankie Laine	1957
Moonlight serenade	Glenn Miller	1954
More	Jimmy Young	1956
		1957

More	Perry Como	1956
More and more party pops	Russ Conway	1959
More party pops	Russ Conway	1958 1959
More than ever (Come prima)	Malcolm Vaughan & The Michael Sammes Singers	1958 1959
Mother Nature and Father Time	Nat 'King' Cole	1953
Mountain greenery	Mel Torme	1956
Move it	Cliff Richard & The Drifters	1958
Mr.Blue	David MacBeth	1959
Mr.Blue	Mike Preston	1959
Mr.Sandman	Chordettes	1954 1955
Mr.Sandman	Dickie Valentine	1954 1955
Mr.Sandman	Four Aces	1955
Mr.Sandman	Max Bygraves	1955
Mr.Wonderful	Peggy Lee	1957
My boy flat top	Frankie Vaughan	1956
My Dixie darling	Lonnie Donegan	1957
My friend	Frankie Laine	1954
My happiness	Connie Francis	1959
My love and devotion	Doris Day	1952
My one sin	Nat 'King' Cole	1955
My prayer	Platters	1956 1957
My September love	David Whitfield	1956
My September love	Joan Regan	1956
My son, my son	Vera Lynn	1954 1955
My special angel	Malcolm Vaughan	1957 1958
My true love	Jack Scott	1958
Nairobi	Tommy Steele	1958
Never be anyone else but you	Ricky Nelson	1959
Never do a tango with an eskimo	Alma Cogan	1955 1956
Night train	Buddy Morrow	1953
No more	McGuire Sisters	1955
No one but you	Billy Eckstine	1954 1955

No other love	Dave King	1956
No other love	Ronnie Hilton	1956
Not as a stranger	Frank Sinatra	1955
Nothin' to do	Michael Holliday	1956
Now	Al Martino	1953
Oh boy!	Buddy Holly & The Crickets	1958
Oh Carol	Neil Sedaka	1959
Oh happy day	Johnston Brothers	1953
Oh mein Papa	Eddie Calvert	1953 1954
Oh my papa	Eddie Fisher	1954
Oh! Suzanna / medley: Pat-a-cake / Three blind mice / Jingle bells	Don Charles' Singing Dogs	1955
Oh-oh I'm falling in love again	Jimmie Rodgers	1958
On the street where you live	David Whitfield	1958
On the street where you live	Vic Damone	1958
On with the motley	Harry Secombe	1955
One more sunrise	Dickie Valentine	1959
One night	Elvis Presley	1959
Only sixteen	Craig Douglas	1959
Only you	Hilltoppers	1956
Only you	Platters	1956 1957
Open up your heart	Joan & Rusty Regan	1955
Out of town	Dickie Valentine	1956
Out of town	Max Bygraves	1956
Outside of Heaven	Eddie Fisher	1953
Papa loves mambo	Perry Como	1954
Paralysed	Elvis Presley	1957
Party	Elvis Presley	1957 1958
Paths of Paradise	Johnnie Ray	1955
Patricia	Perez Prado	1958
Peggy Sue	Buddy Holly & The Crickets	1958
Peggy Sue got married	Buddy Holly & The Crickets	1959
Personality	Anthony Newley	1959
Personality	Lloyd Price	1959
Peter Gunn	Duane Eddy	1959
Petite Fleur	Chris Barber's Jazz Band	1959

Piano medley No. 114	Charlie Kunz	1954
		1955
Piano party	Winifred Atwell	1959
Pickin' a chicken	Eve Boswell	1956
Plenty good lovin'	Connie Francis	1959
Poison Ivy	Coasters	1959
Poor Jenny	Everly Brothers	1959
Poor little fool	Ricky Nelson	1958
Poor people of Paris	Winifred Atwell	1956
Poppa Piccolino	Diana Decker	1953
		1954
Port-Au-Prince	Winifred Atwell & Frank Chaksfield	1956
Portuguese washerwoman	Joe 'Fingers' Carr	1956
Pretend	Nat 'King' Cole	1953
Pretty little black eyed Susie	Guy Mitchell	1953
Prize of gold	Joan Regan	1955
Problems	Everly Brothers	1959
Purple people eater	Sheb Wooley	1958
Put your head on my shoulder	Paul Anka	1959
Puttin' on the style	Billy Cotton	1957
Puttin' on the style	Lonnie Donegan	1957
Rachel	Al Martino	1953
Rags to riches	David Whitfield	1953
		1954
Ragtime Cowboy Joe	David Seville & The Chipmunks	1959
Railroad Bill	Lonnie Donegan	1956
Rain, rain, rain	Frankie Laine & The Four Lads	1954
		1955
Raunchy	Bill Justis	1958
Raunchy	Ken Mackintosh	1958
Rave on	Buddy Holly & The Crickets	1958
Rawhide	Frankie Laine	1959
Razzle dazzle	Bill Haley & His Comets	1956
Ready, willing and able	Doris Day	1955
Real love	Ruby Murray	1958
		1959
Rebel rouser	Duane Eddy	1958
Red River rock	Johnny & The Hurricanes	1959

Reet petite	Jackie Wilson	1957
		1958
Remember you're mine	Pat Boone	1957
		1958
Return to me	Dean Martin	1958
Ricochet	Joan Regan	1953
		1954
Rip it up	Bill Haley & His Comets	1956
		1957
Robin Hood	Dick James with Stephen James & His Chums	1956
Robin Hood	Gary Miller	1956
Rock and roll waltz	Kay Starr	1956
Rock around the clock	Bill Haley & His Comets	1955
		1956
Rock Island line	Lonnie Donegan	1956
Rock this joint	Bill Haley & His Comets	1957
Rock with the caveman	Tommy Steele	1956
Rock-a-beatin' boogie	Bill Haley & His Comets	1956
Rock-a-billy	Guy Mitchell	1957
Rock-a-bye your baby	Jerry Lewis	1957
Rockin' through the rye	Bill Haley & His Comets	1956
		1957
Rose Marie	Slim Whitman	1955
Roulette	Russ Conway	1959
Sally don't grieve	Lonnie Donegan	1958
Sal's got a sugar lip	Lonnie Donegan	1959
San Miguel	Lonnie Donegan	1959
Santa bring my baby back to me	Elvis Presley	1957
		1958
Santo Natale	David Whitfield	1954
		1955
Sat'day night rock-a-boogie	Anthony Newley	1959
Say you're mine again	Jane Hutton & Axel Stordahl	1953
Scarlet ribbons	Harry Belafonte & Millard Thomas	1957
Sea of love	Marty Wilde	1959
Secret love	Doris Day	1954
See you later alligator	Bill Haley & His Comets	1956
Serenade	Mario Lanza	1955
Serenade	Slim Whitman	1956

Seven days	Anne Shelton	1956
Seven little girls (sitting in the back seat)	Avons	1959
Seven lonely days	Gisele McKenzie	1953
Seventeen	Boyd Bennett & His Rockets	1955
Seventeen	Frankie Vaughan	1955
Shake, rattle and roll	Bill Haley & His Comets	1954 1955
Sh-boom	Crew Cuts	1954
Sh-boom	Stan Freberg	1954
She wears red feathers	Guy Mitchell	1953
She's got it	Little Richard	1957
Shiralee	Tommy Steele	1957
Side by side	Kay Starr	1953
Side saddle	Russ Conway	1959
Silent night	Bing Crosby	1952 1953
Sincerely	McGuire Sisters	1955
Sing it again with Joe	Joe 'Mr.Piano' Henderson	1955
Sing it with Joe	Joe 'Mr.Piano' Henderson	1955
Sing little birdie	Pearl Carr & Teddy Johnson	1959
Singing the blues	Guy Mitchell	1956 1957
Singing the blues	Tommy Steele	1956 1957
Sippin' soda	Guy Mitchell	1954
Sixteen tons	Frankie Laine & The Mellomen	1956
Sixteen tons	Tennessee Ernie Ford	1956
Skin deep	Duke Ellington	1954
Skin deep	Ted Heath & His Music	1954
Smile	Nat 'King' Cole	1954
Smoke gets in your eyes	Platters	1959
Snow coach	Russ Conway	1959
Softly, softly	Ruby Murray	1955
Some kind-a-earthquake	Duane Eddy	1959
Somebody	Stargazers	1955
Somebody stole my gal	Johnnie Ray	1953
Someday	Ricky Nelson	1958 1959

Someday (you'll want me to want you)	Jodie Sands	1958
Someone	Johnny Mathis	1959
Someone else's roses	Joan Regan	1954
Someone on your mind	Jimmy Young	1955 1956
Something's gotta give	Sammy Davis Jr.	1955
Somewhere along the way	Nat 'King' Cole	1952 1953
Song of the dreamer	Johnnie Ray	1955
Splish splash	Bobby Darin	1958
Splish splash	Charlie Drake	1958
St.Therese of the Roses	Malcolm Vaughan	1956 1957
Staccato's theme	Elmer Bernstein	1959
Stackalee	Lonnie Donegan	1956
Stagger Lee	Lloyd Price	1959
Stairway of love	Michael Holliday	1958
Stairway of love	Terry Dene	1958
Stardust	Billy Ward & The Dominoes	1957
Stars shine in your eyes	Ronnie Hilton	1955
Start movin' (in my direction)	Sal Mineo	1957
Stewball	Lonnie Donegan	1956
Stowaway	Barbara Lyon	1955
Strange lady in town	Frankie Laine	1955
Stranger in Paradise	Bing Crosby	1955
Stranger in Paradise	Don Cornell	1955
Stranger in Paradise	Eddie Calvert	1955
Stranger in Paradise	Four Aces	1955
Stranger in Paradise	Tony Bennett	1955
Stranger in Paradise	Tony Martin	1955
Stupid cupid	Connie Francis	1958
Such a night	Johnnie Ray	1954
Suddenly there's a valley	Jo Stafford	1955 1956
Suddenly there's a valley	Lee Lawrence	1955
Suddenly there's a valley	Petula Clark	1955 1956
Sugar moon	Pat Boone	1958
Sugarbush	Doris Day & Frankie Laine	1952 1953

Sugartime	Alma Cogan	1958
Sugartime	McGuire Sisters	1958
Summertime blues	Eddie Cochran	1958
Sway	Dean Martin	1954
Swedish Rhapsody	Mantovani Orchestra	1953 1954
Swedish Rhapsody	Ray Martin Concert Orchestra	1953 1954
Sweet little sixteen	Chuck Berry	1958
Sweeter than you	Ricky Nelson	1959
Swingin' shepherd blues	Ella Fitzgerald	1958
Swingin' shepherd blues	Ted Heath & His Music	1958
Take a message to Mary	Everly Brothers	1959
Take my heart	Al Martino	1952
Takes two to tango	Louis Armsrong	1952 1953
Tallahassee Lassie	Freddy Cannon	1959
Tallahassee Lassie	Tommy Steele	1959
Tammy	Debbie Reynolds	1957
Tea for two cha-cha	Tommy Dorsey Orchestra feat. Warren Covington	1958 1959
Teach me tonight	De Castro Sisters	1955
Teen beat	Sandy Nelson	1959
Tell me a story	Frankie Laine & Jimmy Boyd	1953
Tenderly	Nat 'King' Cole	1954
Tennessee wig walk	Bonnie Lou	1954
Tequila	Champs	1958
Terry's theme from 'Limelight'	Frank Chacksfield	1953
Terry's theme from 'Limelight'	Ron Goodwin	1953
That old black magic	Sammy Davis Jr.	1955
That'll be the day	Buddy Holly & The Crickets	1957
That's amore	Dean Martin	1954
That's how a love song was born	Ray Burns & The Coronets	1955
The adoration waltz	David Whitfield	1957
The ballad of Davy Crockett	Bill Hayes	1956
The ballad of Davy Crockett	Dick James with Stephen James & His Chums	1956
The ballad of Davy Crockett	Max Bygraves	1956
The ballad of Davy Crockett	Tennessee Ernie Ford	1956
The banana boat song	Harry Belafonte	1957
The banana boat song	Shirley Bassey	1957

The banana boat song	Tarriers	1957
The banjo's back in town	Alma Cogan	1955
The big beat	Fats Domino	1958
The black hills of Dakota	Doris Day	1954
The book	David Whitfield	1954
The breeze and I	Caterina Valente	1955
The clouds will soon roll by	Tony Brent	1958
The Crazy Otto rag	Stargazers	1955
The creep	Ken Mackintosh	1954
The cuff of my shirt	Guy Mitchell	1954
The day the rains came	Jane Morgan	1958 1959
The drinking song	Mario Lanza	1955
The faithful Hussar	Ted Heath & His Music	1956
The finger of suspicion	Dickie Valentine	1954 1955
The gal with the yaller shoes	Michael Holliday	1956
The gal with the yaller shoes	Michael Holliday	1956
The girl can't help it	Little Richard	1957
The girl in the wood	Frankie Laine	1953
The Grand Coolie dam	Lonnie Donegan	1958
The great pretender	Jimmy Parkinson	1956
The great pretender	Platters	1956 1957
The happy wanderer	Obernkirchen Children's Choir	1954
The happy wanderer	Stargazers	1954
The happy whistler	Don Robertson	1956
The heart of a man	Frankie Vaughan	1959
The homing waltz	Vera Lynn	1952
The Isle of Innisfree	Bing Crosby	1952 1953
The Italian Theme	Cyril Stapleton	1956
The kid's last fight	Frankie Laine	1954
The little shoemaker	Petula Clark	1954
The man from Laramie	Al Martino	1955
The man from Laramie	Jimmy Young	1955
The man that got away	Judy Garland	1955
The naughty lady of Shady Lane	Ames Brothers	1955
The naughty lady of Shady Lane	Dean Martin	1955

The old pianna rag	Dickie Valentine	1955 1956
The only man on the island	Tommy Steele	1958
The Saints rock 'n' roll	Bill Haley & His Comets	1956
The shifting whispering sands	Billy Vaughan Orchestra	1956
The shifting whispering sands	Eamonn Andrews	1956
The son of Mary	Harry Belafonte	1958
The story of my life	Dave King	1958
The story of my life	Gary Miller	1958
The story of my life	Michael Holliday	1958
The story of three loves (Rachmaninoff's 18th variation on a theme by Paganini)	Winifred Atwell	1954
The story of Tina	Al Martino	1954
The story of Tina	Ronnie Harris	1954
The three bells	Browns	1959
The trouble with Harry	Alfi & Harry	1956
The wayward wind	Gogi Grant	1956
The wayward wind	Tex Ritter	1956
The Windsor waltz	Vera Lynn	1953
The wisdom of a fool	Norman Wisdom	1957
The wisdom of a fool	Ronnie Carroll	1957
The wonderful secret of love	Robert Earl	1959
The world outside	Four Aces	1959
The world outside	Ronnie Hilton & The Mike Sammes Singers	1959
The yellow rose of Texas	Gary Miller	1955
The yellow rose of Texas	Mitch Miller	1955 1956
The yellow rose of Texas	Ronnie Hilton	1955
Theme from 'Moulin Rouge'	Mantovani Orchestra	1953
Theme from 'Picnic'	Morris Stoloff	1956
Theme from 'The Army Game'	Original Cast Of The Army Game	1958
Theme from 'The Man With The Golden Arm'	Billy May & His Orchestra	1956
Theme from 'The Threepenny Opera'	Billy Vaughan Orchestra	1956
Theme from 'The Threepenny Opera'	Dick Hyman Trio	1956

Theme from 'The Threepenny Opera'	Louis Armstrong	1956
There must be a reason	Frankie Laine	1954
There's a goldmine in the sky	Pat Boone	1957 1958
Think it over	Buddy Holly & The Crickets	1958
This ole house	Billie Anthony	1954 1955
This ole house	Rosemary Clooney	1954 1955
Three coins in the fountain	Four Aces	1954
Three coins in the fountain	Frank Sinatra	1954
Three stars	Ruby Wright	1959
To be loved	Malcolm Vaughan & The Michael Sammes Singers	1958
To know him is to love him	Teddy Bears	1959
Tom Dooley	Kingston Trio	1958 1959
Tom Dooley	Lonnie Donegan	1958 1959
Tom Hark	Elias & His Zig Zag Jive Flutes	1958
Tomboy	Perry Como	1959
Tomorrow	Johnny Brandon & The Phantoms	1955
Too much	Elvis Presley	1957
Too young to go steady	Nat 'King' Cole	1956
Torero	Julius La Rosa	1958
Travellin' home	Vera Lynn	1957
Travellin' light	Cliff Richard & The Shadows	1959
Trudie	Joe 'Mr.Piano' Henderson	1958
True love	Bing Crosby & Grace Kelly	1956 1957
Trying to get to you	Elvis Presley	1957
Tulips from Amsterdam	Max Bygraves	1958
Tumbling tumbleweeds	Slim Whitman	1956
Tweedle dee	Frankie Vaughan	1955
Tweedle dee	Georgia Gibbs	1955
Twenty tiny fingers	Alma Cogan	1955
Twenty tiny fingers	Coronets	1955

107

Twenty tiny fingers	Stargazers	1955
		1956
Twilight time	Platters	1958
Twixt twelve and twenty	Pat Boone	1959
Two different worlds	Ronnie Hilton	1956
		1957
Unchained melody	Al Hibbler	1955
Unchained melody	Jimmy Young	1955
Unchained melody	Les Baxter & His Orchestra	1955
Unchained melody	Liberace	1955
Under the bridges of Paris	Dean Martin	1955
Under the bridges of Paris	Eartha Kitt	1955
Vanessa	Ted Heath & His Music	1953
Vaya con dios	Les Paul & Mary Ford	1953
Veni vidi vici	Ronnie Hilton	1954
		1955
Venus	Dickie Valentine	1959
Venus	Frankie Avalon	1959
Volare	Dean Martin	1958
Volare	Domenico Modugno	1958
Volare	Marino Marini Quartet	1958
Wait for me	Malcolm Vaughan	1959
Wait for me darling	Joan Regan & The Johnston Brothers	1954
Wake up little Susie	Everly Brothers	1957
		1958
Walk hand in hand	Ronnie Carroll	1956
Walk hand in hand	Tony Martin	1956
Walkin' my baby back home	Johnnie Ray	1952
Walkin' to Missouri	Tony Brent	1952
		1953
Wanderin' eyes	Charlie Gracie	1957
Wanderin' eyes	Frankie Vaughan	1957
Wanted	Al Martino	1954
Wanted	Perry Como	1954
Water water	Tommy Steele	1957
We are not alone	Frankie Vaughan	1958
We will make love	Russ Hamilton	1957
Wear my ring around your neck	Elvis Presley	1958
Wedding ring	Russ Hamilton	1957
Wee Tom	Lord Rockingham's XI	1959

West of Zanzibar	Anthony Steel & the Radio Revellers	1954
Western movies	Olympics	1958
What do you want to make those eyes at me for?	Emile Ford & The Checkmates	1959
What do you want?	Adam Faith	1959
Whatever will be will be (Que sera sera)	Doris Day	1956
When	Kalin Twins	1958
When I fall in love	Jimmy Young	1957
When I fall in love	Nat 'King' Cole	1957
When Mexico gave up the Rhumba	Mitchell Torok	1956 1957
When you lose the one you love	David Whitfield & Mantovani	1955 1956
Where the winds blow	Frankie Laine	1953
Where were you (on our wedding day)?	Lloyd Price	1959
Where will the dimple be?	Rosemary Clooney & The Mellomen	1955
White Christmas	Mantovani Orchestra	1952 1953
Who are we	Ronnie Hilton	1956
Who's sorry now?	Connie Francis	1958
Whole lotta shakin' goin' on	Jerry Lee Lewis	1957
Whole lotta woman	Marvin Rainwater	1958
Who's sorry now?	Johnnie Ray	1956
Why baby why	Pat Boone	1957
Why do fools fall in love	Frankie Lymon & The Teenagers	1956
Why don't you believe me?	Joni James	1953
Willie can	Alma Cogan	1956
Willingly	Malcolm Vaughan	1959
Winifred Atwell	Theme from "A Threepenny Opera"	1956
Winter wonderland	Johnny Mathis	1959
Wish you were here	Eddie Fisher	1953 1954
Witch doctor	David Seville	1958
Witch doctor	Don Lang & His Frantic Five	1958
Witchcraft	Frank Sinatra	1958

With all my heart	Petula Clark	1957
With your love	Malcolm Vaughan	1956
Woman from Liberia	Jimmie Rodgers	1959
Wonderful Copenhagen	Danny Kaye	1953
Yakety Yak	Coasters	1958
Yep!	Duane Eddy	1959
Yes tonight, Josephine	Johnnie Ray	1957
Ying tong song	Goons	1956
You always hurt the one you love	Connie Francis	1959
You are my destiny	Paul Anka	1958
You are my first love	Ruby Murray	1956
You belong to me	Jo Stafford	1952
		1953
You brought a new kind of love to me	Frank Sinatra	1956
You can't be true to two	Dave King & The Keynotes	1956
You don't owe me a thing	Johnnie Ray	1957
You my love	Frank Sinatra	1955
You need hands	Max Bygraves	1958
You, me and us	Alma Cogan	1957
Young and beautiful	Elvis Presley	1958
Young and foolish	Dean Martin	1956
Young and foolish	Edmund Hockridge	1956
Young and foolish	Ronnie Hilton	1956
Young at heart	Frank Sinatra	1954
Young love	Sonny James	1957
Young love	Tab Hunter	1957
You're getting to be a habit with me	Frank Sinatra	1956
You're the top cha cha	Al Saxon	1959
Zambesi	Eddie Calvert	1956
Zambesi	Lou Busch	1956
Zing a little zong	Bing Crosby & Jane Wyman	1952

eferences:

BBC On This Day – 15 August

"King George opens Festival of Britain". *BBC News*. 3 May 1951. Archived from the original on 7 March 2008. etrieved 2008-02-03

"Churchill wins general election". *BBC News*. 26 October 1951. Archived from the original on 7 March 2008. etrieved 2008-02-03

"The Lawn". *Images of England*. English Heritage. Retrieved 20 June 2010

The Lawn, Harlow Essex". *Heritage Explorer*. English Heritage. Retrieved 2012-11-12

"Redeveloping Essex's fallen utopia". *BBC News*. 16 January 2007. Retrieved 20 June 2010

ttp://en.wikipedia.org/wiki/1950_in_the_United_Kingdom

The Lost Decade Timeline, BBC" Retrieved 2008-01-29

Results: Saturday 19th August 1950". *Statto.com*. Retrieved 2013-05-13

"History". Port Vale F.C. Retrieved 2013-05-13

"1951".*www.fa-cupfinals.co.uk*. Retrieved 2011-01-01

"Soccer moguls drop one team". *Leader-post* (Regina)). 2 June 1951. p.17. Retrieved 2013-04-17

Kynaston, David (2007). *Austerity Britain 1945-1951.*London: Bloomsbury. ISBN 978-0-7475-7985-4

"The Lost Decade Timeline, BBC" Retrieved 2008-02-03

Penguin Pocket On This Day. Penguin Reference Library. 2006. ISBN 0-14-102715-0.

The Hutchinson Factfinder. Helicon. 1999. ISBN 1-85986-000-1

Meisner, Nadine (3 December 2004). "Dame Alicia Markova". *The Independent*. trieved 2010-06-10

"Lucy Barfield: The Real Lucy of Narnia". *Into the Wardrobe*. 27 May 2006. Retrieved 2010-10-04

ttps://en.wikipedia.org/wiki/1951_in_the_United_States

Palmer, Alan;Veronica (1992). *The Chronology of British History*. London: Century Ltd. pp. 401-402. ISBN 0-7126-16-2

Lavington, Simon (1998). *A History of Manchester Computers (2nd ed.)* Swindon: British Computer Society. ISBN 8-0-902505-01-8

Gregory, Helen (3 November 2001). "It's a super anniversary". *The Grocer*. Retrieved 2011-04-19

Ferry, Georgina (2004). "4". *A Computer Called LEO: Lyons Tea Shops and the World's First Office Computer*. ndon: Harper Perennial. ISBN 1-84115-186-6

"UK drivers cheer end of fuel rations". *BBC News*. 26 May 1950. Archived from the original on March 7 2008. trieved 2008-01-29

Penguin Pocket On This Day. Penguin Reference Library. 2006. ISBN 0-14-102715-0

"London fog clears after days of chaos". *On This Day*. BBC. 9 December 1952. Archived from the original on 24 tober 2007. Retrieved 2007-12-04

ttp://en.wikipedia.org/wiki/1952_in_the_United_Kingdom

"History". *Cairngorm Reindeer Herd*. Reindeer Company. Archived from the original on 22 July 2010. Retrieved 0-07-16

"Prescription Charges" (PDF). Royal Pharmaceutical Society, 2009. Retrieved 2010-06-13

Kynaston, David (2009). *Family Britain 1951-57*. London: Bloomsbury. ISBN 978-0-7475-8385-1

ttps://en.wikipedia.org/wiki/list_of_FA-Cup_finals

New Ambassadors Theatre" *arthurlloyd.co.uk*. Archived from the original on 9 November 2007. Retrieved 2007-04

Test drive for TV detector vans". *On This Day*. BBC.1 February 1952. Archived from the original on 27 December 7. Retrieved 2007-12-04

Tea rationing to end". *On This Day*. BBC. 3 October 1952. Retrieved 2007-12-04

Palmer, Alan; Veronica (1992) *The Chronology of British History*. London. Century Ltd. pp. 404-405. ISBN 0-7126-6-2

The Hutchinson Factfinder. Helicon. 1999. ISBN 1-85986-000-1

Marshall, Prince (1972). *Wheels of London*. The Sunday Times Magazine. pp. 80, 93-96. ISBN 0-7230-0068-9

Palmer, Alan; Veronica (1992). *The Chronology of British History*. London: Century Ltd. pp. 406-407. ISBN 0-6-5616-2

Penguin Pocket On This Day. Penguin Reference Library. 2006. ISBN 0-14-102715-0

Sweet rationing ends in Britain." *BBC On This Day*. 5 February 1953. Archived from the original on 25 December 7. Retrieved 10 January 2008

ttp://www.manutd.com/en/Players-And-Staff/Legends/Tommy-Taylor:aspx?pageNo=2

ttp://www.munich58.co.uk/memorabilia/books/taylor.asp

[43] http://www.fa-cupfinals.co.uk/1953.html

[44] Marr, Andrew (2007). *A History of Modern Britain*. London. Macmillan. p.87. ISBN 978-1-4050-0538-8

[45] Gallagher, Brendan (4 June 2011). "1953: A golden year for sport". *The Daily Telegraph*. Retrieved 4 June 2011.

[46] "The Lost Decade Timeline, BBC". Retrieved 10 January 2008

[47] "Lords vote for commercial television".*BBC On This Day*. 26 November 1953. Archived from the original on 28 November 2007. Retrieved 10 January 2008.

[48] Lambert, Tim. "Britain since 1948". Retrieved 3 April 2013

[49] http://en.wikipedia.org/wiki/1953_in_the_United_Kingdom

[50] "The Coming of the Cafes: 1953…" *Classic Cafes*. 1999-2008. Retrieved 12 July 2010

[51] "Queen launches Royal Yacht Britannia". *BBC On This Day*.16 April 1953. Archived from the original on 21 January 2008. Retrieved 10 January 2008

[52] *"Dinard-Viking"*. *Simplon Postcards: The Passenger Ship Website*. 2005. Retrieved 22 October 2012

[53] "Three continents see eclipse of sun". *On This Day*. BBC News. 30 June 1954. Retrieved 2012-11-12

[54] "The Lost Decade Timeline, BBC". Retrieved 2008-02-06

[55] "Bannister breaks four-minute mile". *On This Day*. BBC News. 6 May 1954. Archived from the original on 7 Marc 2008. Retrieved 2008-02-06

[56] "Oxford wins 100th Boat Race". *On This Day*. BBC News. 3 April 1954. Archived from the original on 7 March 2008. Retrieved 2008-02-06

[57] *World Football Legends* homepage

[58] "Chataway beats 5,000m world record". *On This Day*. BBC News. 13 October 1954. Archived from the original on March 2008. Retrieved 2008-02-06

[59] http://en.wikipedia.org/wiki/1954_in_the_United_Kingdom

[60] "Diane Leather". *Sporting Heroes*. Retrieved 2012-11-12

[61] "50 years ago Roger Bannister became a sporting legend with his four-minute mile: Why is his female equivalent j seen as an also-ran?". *The Independent* (London).

[62] "The Grove Family". *Whirligig*. Archived from the original on 10 August 2010. Retrieved 2010-07-05

[63] http://en.wikipedia.org/wiki/1954_in_British_Music

[64] "Housewives celebrate end of rationing". *On This Day*. BBC News. 4 July 1954. Archived from the original on 7 March 2008. Retrieved 2008-02-06

[65] "Wimpy Moments". Wimpy. 2010. Archived from the original on 28 March 2010. Retrieved 2010-07-01.

[66] "New authority for atomic energy". *On This Day*. BBC News. 12 February 1954. Archived from the original on 7 March 2008. Retrieved 2008-02-06

[67] Berry, George (1970). *Discovering Schools*. Tring: Shire Publications ISBN 0-85263-091-3

[68] *Penguin Pocket On This Day*. Penguin Reference Library. 2006. ISBN 0-14-102715-0.

[69] "Capital claims – A city's struggle". *BBC News*. 22 April 2003. Retrieved 2011-02-07

[70] "Britain's big freeze". *BBC News*. 24 February 1955. Retrieved 2009-12-05

[71] "Trophy – 1955 League Title". *Chelseaafc.com*. Chelsea Football Club. 11 July 2002. Retrieved 2012-02-10

[72] "1955". *The FA Cup*. Archived from the original on 22 May 2010. Retrieved 2011-02-04

[73] "Moss claims first Grand Prix victory". *BBC News*. 17 July 1955. Archived from the original on 7 March 2008. Retrieved 2008-02-11

[74] "Duncan Edwards: A prodigious talent cut down in his prime". *Mirror Football. Daily Mirror*. Retrieved 2012-02-

[75] "The Lost Decade Timeline, BBC". Retrieved 2008-02-11

[76] "New TV channel ends BBC monopoly". *.BBC News*. 22 September 1955. Archived from the original on 7 March 2008. Retrieved 2008-02-11

[77] http://en.wikipedia.org/wiki/1955_in_British_Music

[78] http://en.wikipedia.org/wiki/1955_in_the_United_Kingdom

[79] Pietrobon, Steven S. (24 June 2005). "Airfix's First Aircraft Kit: The Spitfire BTK". Retrieved 2010-11-06

[80] Parkinson, C. Northcote (19 November 1955) "Parkinson's Law". *The Economist*. Retrieved 5 October 2010

[81] *Penguin Pocket On This Day*. Penguin Reference Library. 2006. ISBN 0-14-102715-0

[82] "Gower national park status call". BBC News. 9 May 2006. Retrieved 2010-01-31

[83] Palmer, Alan; Veronica (1992). *The Chronology of British History*. London. Century Ltd. pp. 410-411. ISBN 0-7126-5616-2

[84] Robertson, Patrick (1974). *The Shell Book of Firsts*. London: Ebury Press. p.243. ISBN 0-7181-1279-2

[85] "Macmillan unveils premium bond scheme". *BBC News*. 18 April 1956. Retrieved 2012-02-13

[86] Weinreb, Ben; Christopher Hibbert (1995), *The London Encyclopaedia*. London: Macmillan. ISBN 0-333-57688-8

[87] "France and UK considered 1950's merger". *The Guardian* (London). 16 January 2007. Archived from the origina on 19 November 2007. Retrieved 2007-12-04

"Manchester United Clinches First Division Soccer Title". *Saskatoon Star-Phoenix*. 9 April 1956. Retrieved 2012-
∎-13

http://en.wikipedia.org/wiki/1956_in_the_United_Kingdom

https://en.wikipedia.org/wiki/1956_in_British_music

"Corgi History". Retrieved 2010-08-17

"Sellafield Sites, Site History". Retrieved 2007-12-04

"Tesco Plc: Overview." Archived from the original on 30 July 2007. Retrieved 2007-08-17

"Tesco: Our History." www.tescocorporate.com. Tesco plc. Retrieved 2007-03-27

"Brothers Frank and Also Berni revolutionised how we ate out with their Temperance Bars". *Western Daily Press*. istol. 2014-05-13. Retrieved 2015-03-28

Penguin Pocket On This Day. Penguin Reference Library. 2006. ISBN 0-14-102715-0

"Motorists panic as petrol rations loom". *On This Day*. BBC. 29 November 1956. Archived from the original on 15 cember 2007. Retrieved 2007-12-04

"Our Computer Heritage." Computer Conservation Society. 4 March 2012. Retrieved 2012-04-07

"Manchester United retains soccer supremacy." *Leader-Post* (Regina, Saskatchewan). 22 April 1957. p.19. Retrieved 12-12-10

http://www.fa-cupfinals.co.uk/1957.htm

"Grand Prix Results: British GP, 1957". Grandprix.com. Retrieved 2012-07-07

South v North in 1957

http://en.wikipedia.org/wiki/1957_in_the_United_Kingdom

"BBC fools the nation." *BBC News*. 1 April 1957. Retrieved 2007-12-04

Penguin Pocket On This Day. Penguin Reference Library. 2006. ISBN 0-14-102715-0

http://en-wikipedia.org/wiki/1957_in_British_Music

"Cheers as petrol rationing ended". *BBC News*. 14 May 1957. Retrieved 2007-12-04

Penguin Pocket On This Day. Penguin Reference Library. 2006. ISBN 0-14-102715-0

"A Changing House: the Life Peerages Act 1958". Archived from the original on 15 June 2008. Retrieved 2008-03-

Leach, Nicholas (2003). *Oakley Class Lifeboats: an Illustrated History of the RNLI's Oakley and Rother Lifeboats*. oud: Tempus. ISBN 978-0-7524-2784-3

http://en.wikipedia.org/wiki/1958_in_the_United_Kingdom

http://en-wikipedia.org/wiki/1958_in_British_music

"Events in Telecommunications History – 1958". Retrieved 2008-01-27

"Carnaby Street". www.retrowow.co.uk. Archived from the original on 1 March 2009. Retrieved 2009-02-22

"1958". CBRD

"Norwich to use postal codes – Experimenting in automation", *The Times*, 29 July 1959

"1959: Fog brings transport chaos". *BBC News*. 29 January 1959. Retrieved 2009-07-02

"June anniversaries". *The BBC Story*. BBC. Archived from the original on 28 January 2011. Retrieved 2011-03-03

http://en.wikipedia.org/wiki/1959_in_the_United_Kingdom

"1959". *Those were the days*. Wolverhampton: *Express & Star*. Retrieved 2014-07-23

"Cow & Gate Limited". *The Times*. 1 April 1959

"1959: Harrods in £34 million merger talks". *BBC News*. 22 June 1959. Retrieved 2009-07-02

"Outsider who changed the City".*Management Today*. 1 November 1998. Retrieved 2010-07-09

"1959: Hovercraft marks new era in transport". *BBC News*. 11 June 1959. Archived from the original on 6 January)8. Retrieved 2008-02-05

Penguin Pocket On This Day. Penguin Reference Library. 2006. ISBN 0-14-102715-0

"Chronology of Scottish History". *ATimeline of Scottish History*. Rampant Scotland. Retrieved 2014-07-23

Printed in Great Britain
by Amazon